FDI
and
Development
in
Vietnam

The **Institute of Southeast Asian Studies (ISEAS)** was established as an autonomous organization in 1968. It is a regional centre dedicated to the study of socio-political, security and economic trends and developments in Southeast Asia and its wider geostrategic and economic environment.

The Institute's research programmes are the Regional Economic Studies (RES, including ASEAN and APEC), Regional Strategic and Political Studies (RSPS), and Regional Social and Cultural Studies (RSCS).

ISEAS Publications, an established academic press, has issued more than 1,000 books and journals. It is the largest scholarly publisher of research about Southeast Asia from within the region. ISEAS Publications works with many other academic and trade publishers and distributors to disseminate important research and analyses from and about Southeast Asia to the rest of the world.

FDI and Development in Vietnam

Policy Implications

Pham Hoang Mai

ISEAS Institute of Southeast Asian Studies
       Singapore

First published in Singapore in 2004 by
Institute of Southeast Asian Studies
30 Heng Mui Keng Terrace
Pasir Panjang
Singapore 119614
http://bookshop.iseas.edu.sg

All rights reserved. No part of this publication may be reproduced, stored in a retrieval system, or transmitted in any form or by any means, electronic, mechancial, photocopying, recording or otherwise, without the prior permission of the Institute of Southeast Asian Studies.

© 2004 Institute of Southeast Asian Studies, Singapore

The responsibility for facts and opinions expressed in this publication rests exclusively with the author whose interpretations do not necessarily reflect the views or the policy of the Institute.

ISEAS Library Cataloguing-in-Publication Data

Pham Hoang Mai
   Foreign direct investment and development in Vietnam : policy implications.
   1. Investments, Foreign—Vietnam.
   2. Vietnam—Economic conditions.
   3. Vietnam—Economic policy—1975–
   I. Title.
HG5750.5 A3P53   2004   sls2003021261

ISBN 981-230-225-5

Printed by Markono Printmedia Pte Ltd
Typeset by International Typesetters Pte Ltd

This book is dedicated to my parents, Pham Xuan Phong and Hoang Thi Nguyet, my wife To Minh Huong, and my daughters Pham Huong Nhung and Pham Huong Lien.

Contents

Tables	viii
Figures	x
Acknowledgements	xi
Glossary	xii
1 Introduction	1
2 Theoretical Overview of Foreign Direct Investment	4
3 Socio-Economic Reforms and FDI in Vietnam	19
4 The Macroeconomic Impact of FDI in Vietnam	37
5 Foreign Direct Investment and the Industrialization Process in Vietnam	69
6 FDI, Vietnam's Regional Development and Poverty Alleviation	98
7 Policy Implications	122
8 Conclusion	130
Appendix 1: Regression Analysis on Export Performance of Foreign Invested Enterprises, 1995–98	136
Appendix 2: Regression Analysis on Foreign Invested Enterprises' Performance, 1998	141
Appendix 3: Regression Analysis on Provincial Allocation of Foreign Direct Investment, 1988–98	145
Bibliography	153
Index	169

Tables

3.1	Major Indicators of Macroeconomic Performance of the Vietnamese Economy, 1986–98	20
3.2	Overview of Foreign Direct Investment Flows in Vietnam, 1988–98	23
3.3	Foreign Direct Investment Commitment and Implementation by Forms of Investment, 1988–98	25
3.4	Top 10 Countries Classified by Foreign Direct Investment Commitment, 1988–98	27
3.5	Vietnam's Average Wage Levels, 1996	30
3.6	Japanese Corporations' Reasons for Investing Overseas	31
4.1	Structure of Capital Formation as Percentage of GDP, 1988–98	38
4.2	Vietnam: Balance of Payments, 1988–98	41
4.3	Contribution to Legal Capital, 1988–98	43
4.4	Problems for the Development of Private Enterprises	48
4.5	Major Indicators of Industrial Enterprises, 1995 and 1998	51
4.6	Industrial Output Growth Rate, 1989–98	51
4.7	Share of FIPs' Exports and Imports in Total Exports and Imports of Vietnam, 1991–99	56
4.8	Foreign Loans Classified by Form of Investment, 1991–98	58
4.9	Contribution of Foreign Direct Investment to GDP Growth	62
4.10	Major Industrial Products, 1995–98	64

5.1	Major Indicators of Vietnam's Industry, 1995–98	72
5.2	Vietnam's GDP and Output Structure, 1990–98	77
5.3	Structure of Vietnam's Industrial Output and Capital, 1994–98	79
5.4	Sectoral Revealed Comparative Advantages and Foreign Direct Investment Flows	81
5.5	Foreign Invested Enterprises' Contribution to Total Industrial Capital and Output, 1994 and 1998	91
6.1	Regions in Vietnam: General Indicators	100
6.2	Provincial Allocation of Foreign Direct Investment in Vietnam, 1988–98	102
6.3	Structure of Regional Industrial Output, 1995–98	109
6.4	Social Indicators of Vietnam, 1993–98	111
6.5	Regional Poverty Situation in Vietnam, 1993 and 1998	112
6.6	Labour Working in Foreign Invested Projects, 1994–96	114
6.7	Labour Force Classified by Qualification, 1995	117
6.8	Monthly Income of Labour Working in Foreign Invested Projects	118

Figures

4.1	Gross Domestic Investment and Foreign Direct Investment as Percentage Share of GDP, 1988–98	39
Box 1	Sectors Excluded from Establishing 100 Percent Foreign-Owned Enterprises	49
Box 2	Industrial Products, 80 Percent of the Output of which must be Exported	50
4.2	The Growth Rate of Industrial Capital Outlay of Major Industries, 1994–98	52
4.3	Vietnam's Budgetary Contribution, 1990–98	60
5.1	Contribution to Industrial Growth in Major Industries, 1994–98	80
Box 3	Priority Industrial Investment Projects	90
6.1	Vietnam's Regions and Growth Triangles	99
6.2	Structure of Committed Foreign Direct Investment, 1988–98	104
Box 4	Vietnam's Commitment under AFTA Common Effective Preferential Tariff Scheme	127

Acknowledgements

In the process of completing this book, I have received invaluable help from several people. In particular, I would like to thank Professor John Overton and Dr. Donovan Storey of Massey University, New Zealand, for their constant encouragement and many useful comments.

My special thanks are also due to Associate Professor Gerald Tan, Flinders University of South Australia, for inspiring me to become interested in the topic of development economics and giving me invaluable comments. I wish to express my appreciation to Dr. Suiwah Leung and her colleagues at the Asia Pacific School of Economics and Government, the Australian National University, for assisting me in selecting the appropriate econometric model and for useful advice.

This book is based on my PhD thesis with funding from the NZODA Postgraduate Scholarship granted by the Ministry of Foreign Affairs and Trade of New Zealand. I am grateful to the following publishers for permission to use portions of my work published elsewhere: Blackwell Publishing for permission to reproduce major parts of Chapters 3 and 4 which first appeared in Pham, H.M. "The Socio-Economic Impact of Foreign Direct Investment Flows in Vietnam: 1988–98", *Asian Studies Review* 27, no. 1 (2003): 81–98; Taylor & Francis for permission to reproduce major parts of Chapter 6 which first appeared in Pham, H.M. "Regional Economic Development and Foreign Direct Investment Flows in Vietnam 1988–1998", *Journal of the Asia Pacific Economy* 7, no. 2 (2002): 182–202.

I also wish to express my gratitude for the tremendous support of my parents and my special Kiwi supporters, Paul and Wivian. Finally, my biggest thanks are to my wife Huong, and our dear daughters, Nhung and Lien for giving me the encouragement, advice and motivation to complete this book.

While thanking all the above for the help that they have given me, I hasten to add that this book does not reflect the opinions of any other person, organization or agency and the final responsibility for the content of the book rests with me alone.

Glossary

$	United States dollar
AFTA	ASEAN Free Trade Area
APEC	Asian Pacific Economic Co-operation
ASEAN	Association of Southeast Asian Nations
BCC	business co-operation contract
BOP	balance of payments
BOT	build-operation-transfer
BT	build-transfer
BTO	build-transfer-operation
CU	customs union
DFI	direct foreign investment
EC	European Community
EOI	export-oriented industrialization
EPZs	export processing zones
EU	European Union
FDI	foreign direct investment
FIEs	foreign invested enterprises
FIPs	foreign invested projects
FTA	free trade area
GDP	gross domestic product
GNP	gross national product
GOV	Government of Vietnam
GSO	General Statistical Office
ICOR	incremental capital output ratio

IMF	International Monetary Fund
IOCR	incremental output capital ratio
ISI	import substitution industrialization
ISO	International Organization for Standardization
IZ	industrial zone
MNC	multinational corporation
MOSTE	Ministry of Science, Technology and Environment
MOT	Ministry of Trade
MPI	Ministry of Planning and Investment
NIC	newly industrializing country
ODA	official development assistance
SOE	state-owned enterprises
SRV	Socialist Republic of Vietnam
TNC	transnational corporation
UNDP	United Nations Development Program
VND	Vietnam Dong
VTA	Vietnam Tourism Authority

1
Introduction

Foreign Direct Investment (FDI) to Vietnam between 1988 and 1998 is considered by many observers and policymakers to have played a critical role in the country's transition from a centrally planned to a market-oriented economy. As a result of the government's socio-economic reforms which started in 1986, annual committed FDI flows in Vietnam increased from zero in 1988 to $8.6 billion in 1996, making Vietnam the second biggest recipient of FDI in the world, calculated as a percentage of the gross national product (World Bank 1997a, p. 17). Foreign Direct Investment flows not only to Vietnam but also to many other developing countries, making use of their comparative advantages of cheap labour and natural resources. Arguably, as a result of FDI, many developing countries, such as the newly industrializing countries (NICs) of Asia, have achieved the status of middle-income industrialized economies.

There is debate, however, about whether FDI is useful or detrimental to development and what governments can do to make the most of such investment. These debates tend to fall into two camps—what will be referred to in this book as the mainstream and radical views of the impact of FDI on socio-economic development.

The mainstream view is that in several developing countries, especially in Asia's NICs, FDI flows have covered the savings–investment, foreign exchange, technological and fiscal gaps, and hence promoted economic growth. Foreign Direct Investment flows in these countries have also brought modern technology and management skills that have improved competitiveness and promoted industrialization. It has been argued that high economic growth and changes in economic structure as well as the industrialization process also provide backward and forward linkages to alleviate poverty and income inequality in developing countries in the long term.

In contrast, the radical view points to cases where FDI has had a detrimental effect on socio-economic development. The argument is that FDI has not supplemented, but substituted, domestic savings, thus causing a deterioration in the balance of payments in recipient developing countries. FDI has also been criticized for failing to address poverty in developing countries because it tends to introduce capital-intensive technology that reduces, rather than generates, employment.

This book analyzes the empirical evidence from Vietnam's FDI experience over a ten year period to examine the arguments of both proponents and critics of FDI. In particular, it analyzes the role of the government of Vietnam in promoting and utilizing FDI flows.

This is the first attempt to provide a detailed analysis and insight into the operations and contribution of FDI in Vietnam between 1988 and 1998. The analysis demonstrates that, under the unique conditions of an economy in transition, the government of Vietnam has intervened appropriately to maximize the positive and minimize the harmful effects of FDI, especially with regards to gross national savings and investments, foreign exchange earnings, economic growth, industrialization and poverty alleviation. Based on this analysis, the book will draw some policy implications for FDI mobilization and management in the future.

The data used to analyze the contribution of foreign direct investment to socio-economic development in Vietnam come from several sources. The general data on the socio-economic development of Vietnam and FDI flows to Vietnam over the 1988–98 period come from official publications such as Vietnam's statistical yearbooks, reports of international organizations such as the World Bank, International Monetary Fund, Asian Development Bank, and the United Nations Development Program. Data on the performance of individual foreign direct investment projects come from the databases of pertinent agencies. Such data have been collected through the quarterly survey of foreign direct investment projects. However, given the low level of reliability of such data, extra caution has been used in interpreting them.

Nevertheless, as this book is the first attempt to analyze this wealth of data using both descriptive and regression analyses, it should provide useful insights into the operation and contribution of FDI in Vietnam. In broader terms, it is hoped that this book will contribute to the global debate on the role of FDI in transitional economies and to the discussion on the role of government intervention in mobilizing and utilizing such investment.

This book consists of eight chapters as follows:

Chapter 2 examines several theories about the nature, motivation and impact of FDI flows, outlining both the mainstream and radical views about the role of FDI on socio-economic development. This chapter also reviews the literature on the role of government in attracting FDI and maximizing its positive effects. The relationship between economic integration and FDI flows will also be analyzed.

Chapter 3 sets the context of the Vietnam case study. It reviews socio-economic development in Vietnam since the reforms began in 1986 as well as the volume and structure of FDI flows during the 1988–98 period.

Chapter 4 examines the impact of FDI on domestic savings, gross national investment, foreign exchange earnings, the budget, as well as on economic growth in Vietnam between 1988 and 1998.

Chapter 5 then looks at the contribution of FDI flows to industrialization in Vietnam by examining the role of FDI flows in transferring modern technology, and in promoting the government's dual strategy of export-oriented and import substitution industrialization. There is also a discussion of government policies that have influenced the contribution of FDI to industrialization.

Chapter 6 examines the impact of FDI on Vietnam's regional development and poverty alleviation efforts by analyzing the factors influencing the regional allocation of FDI, and consequent effects on economic growth and employment generation.

Based on the findings of the previous chapters, Chapter 7 generalizes several policy implications that can be used to maximize the positive impact and minimize the detrimental effects of FDI flows in Vietnam in the future. Those policy implications will be very important for boosting FDI flows to Vietnam that started to decline after 1997 as a consequence of the regional financial crisis.

Chapter 8 will return to, and reassess, the mainstream and radical views about the role and impact of FDI in development as well as the role of government in making use of FDI. The main conclusion is that FDI flows may generate either useful or detrimental effects on the economies of developing countries, depending on the government policies. In the case of Vietnam, FDI flows between 1988 and 1998 had a positive effect on socio-economic development, thanks to appropriate government policies.

2
Theoretical Overview of FDI

While FDI is acknowledged as a significant form of capital in many developing economies, often constituting a large proportion of gross national investment, its socio-economic impact is hotly debated. This chapter reviews the various, often oppositional, theories about the nature, origins and patterns of transnational FDI flows. In addition, this chapter analyzes the role of government in influencing the effects of FDI on recipient economies. The arguments presented here set the background for this book's analysis of the impact of the first decade of FDI flows in Vietnam, between 1988 and 1998.

Definitions

There are several ways to define foreign direct investment. According to the International Monetary Fund, FDI includes:

- new equity purchased or acquired by parent companies in overseas firms they are considered to control (including the establishment of new subsidiaries);
- reinvestment of earnings by controlled firms; and
- intra-company loans from parent companies to controlled firms. (Graham and Krugman 1993, p. 16).

The United Nations defines FDI as "an investment involving a long term relationship and reflecting a lasting interest of a resident entity (individual or business) in one economy (direct investor) in an entity resident in an economy other than that of the investor (host country)" (United Nations 1992 cited in Lindblad 1997, p. 1).

In general, FDI has been defined as the long-term investment made by non-residents of a host country through the creation or acquisition of capital assets in the host country. FDI implies the ownership of capital assets large enough to have full or partial control of the enterprise and a physical presence by foreign firms or individuals (Gillis et al. 1992,

p. 374; Hogendorn 1992, p. 414). In this sense, FDI includes not only the transfer of investment capital, but also a whole package of physical capital, modern technology, techniques of production, managerial and marketing knowledge and business practices (Gillis et al. 1992, p. 285; Thirwall 1994, p. 328).

These definitions of FDI show the difference between FDI and portfolio investment in that the latter is the purchase of a host country's bonds or stock by foreigners, but does not involve a controlling ownership (Gillis et al. 1992, p. 374; Hogendorn 1995, p. 414; Meyer and Qu 1995, p. 1). Compared to commercial loans, FDI appears more attractive to developing countries because it involves a risk-sharing relationship with foreign investors (Fry 1997, p. 511).

Foreign direct investment in developing countries can take several forms depending on the conditions of host countries and foreign investors, on the nature of the projects involved, and on the relative bargaining positions of both recipient countries and foreign investors. Nevertheless, FDI tend to take the following forms:

- wholly-owned foreign subsidiaries, in which the ownership is entirely in the hands of foreign firms;
- joint ventures, in which a foreign firm shares ownership with a local partner;
- 'fading-out' agreements, in which local partners will gradually take over the management and ownership of existing foreign investments as their capacities increase;
- licensing of technology;
- franchising of products and brands (such as McDonalds);
- management contracts, in which a foreign firm runs the company with little or no equity share;
- turn-key ventures, in which foreign firms hand over projects to the host country after starting up; and
- production-sharing agreements, in which a foreign firm and local partner share production rather than ownership. (Oman 1984 cited in Chen 1994, p.10; Gillis et al. 1992, pp. 391–2).

Theoretical framework

Several theories have been developed to explain the nature, motives and impact of FDI, including Vernon's product life cycle model; the industrial organization approach; the transaction cost or internalization theory; and Dunning's eclectic theory. In addition, the operations of FDI flows and their impact on recipient developing economies have been interpreted as either highly beneficial and positive (that is, the mainstream view) or conversely, as largely negative (that is, the radical view).

Vernon's Product Life Cycle model

Vernon developed the product life cycle model to explain the evolution of a product in international trade, from being an export item to being produced out of direct investment overseas. The model includes three phases:

- *The early or development phase:* In this phase, the initial demand is small compared to potential demand, production is skilled and labour (rather than capital) intensive, producing a small output for the home market.
- *The growth phase:* In this phase, the demand for new products is expanded in both home and international markets. Production techniques become standardized and tend toward large-scale and long-run production. Part of the product produced domestically is exported to meet foreign demand. Some overseas investment by innovating firms will start to meet international demand.
- *The mature phase:* In this phase, demand in the innovating market is fully met, production technology becomes standardized and during this phase, overseas investment by innovating and foreign firms is likely to peak (Parry 1980, pp. 27–8).

International Organization Theory

International organization theory was first used by Hymer (1960) to explain the movement of FDI in response not to higher interest rates but to financing and supporting the international operations of firms. According to Hymer, the operation of firms abroad is determined by firm-specific advantages such as a firm's market position, patents, access to export markets and to credit, and technological advantages (Frischtak and Newfarmer 1996, p. 297). On the other hand, market structure or country specific characteristics also decide the location of FDI activities. The country specific characteristics can be the cost of labour, the availability of raw materials, energy and capital or population size and GNP per capita (Santiago 1987).

The transaction cost or internalization approach

The transaction cost (or internalization) approach explains FDI as a response to market imperfection. This theory explains FDI as a way for multinational corporations (MNCs) to minimize their transaction costs caused by market imperfection by internalizing their economic activities. Through FDI, structural market imperfections such as tariffs or subsidies, income taxes, import restrictions, foreign exchange controls and other regulatory restrictions can be internalized by multinational corporations. Market imperfection also imposes transaction costs on the transfer of intangible assets such as technology. In order to overcome this problem, MNCs invest in overseas markets instead of selling or licensing their technology or patents (Vernon 1966 cited in Sun 1998, p. 5; Caves 1982; Rugman 1986).

Dunning's Eclectic Theory

According to Dunning's theory, there are three sets of factors that determine foreign direct investment.

- *ownership advantages* include marketing, research and development, or production skills that allow firms to provide goods and services more competitively in their own and other countries.
- *location advantages* include natural resources, domestic market potential, labour, political stability and government policies. These advantages are the main reasons why firms choose to invest in one country rather than another.
- *transaction costs* explain why foreign and local firms choose to combine ownership advantages and location advantages through an internalizing process to overcome different transaction costs (such as transport, tax and other tariffs) or other market imperfections. (Dunning and Narula 1996, pp. 1–2; Bishop 1997, p. 11).

It is argued that countries tend to go through five stages of investment, either to be outward and/or inward direct investors, depending on the changes amongst the three sets of factors mentioned above.

The mainstream view of FDI

The mainstream view is an adaptation of classical economic theory and emphasizes the connection between FDI and economic growth, capital accumulation, promoting free market and laissez-faire economics, free trade policies, open markets and individual decision-making.

Rooted in the Hecksher-Ohlin-Samuelson model, it is argued that international movements of factors of production, including FDI, are decided by the availabilities of primary production inputs in different countries. Foreign direct investment thus moves from countries with low marginal productivity where capital is relatively abundant to countries with higher marginal productivity where capital is relatively scarce. This view is based on assumptions of a perfectly competitive market and identical production functions in different countries as well as identical FDI movement in response to interest rates differences (Bos et al. 1974; Lall and Streeten 1977, pp. 17–18). Thus, FDI flows benefit both source and host countries.

Arguments about the role of FDI in promoting socio-economic development are built on the gaps and the Harrod-Domar models.

8 *Foreign Direct Investment and Development in Vietnam*

According to this view, FDI solves the three major constraints faced by developing economies: the savings–investment, foreign exchange and fiscal gaps. Besides these gaps, there is a likelihood that developing countries face skills shortages (Chenery and Strout 1966; Chenery and Cater 1973; Papanek 1973; Dowling and Hiemenz 1983; Cassen 1986; Mosley 1987; Bacha 1990; White 1992).

The mainstream view argues that FDI flows cover the savings–investment gap, foreign exchange gap, technological gap and fiscal gap in developing countries. Based on the Harrod-Domar model, with decreased Incremental Capital Output Ratio (ICOR) and increased national gross investment resulting from FDI flows, economic growth rate increases[1] (World Bank 1997a, p. 165). Furthermore, FDI also brings in up-to-date technology and management skills that help to improve a country's competitiveness, and promote industrialization.

Finally, mainstream theorists hold that FDI-driven high economic growth, changing economic structures and industrialization also provide backward and forward effects that alleviate poverty and income inequality in developing countries.

The radical view of FDI

The radical view lies largely within the neo-Marxist paradigm and includes not only Dependency Theory but also other views that could be classified as "anti-establishment". Unlike the mainstream view, the radical view, especially Dependency Theory, focuses on the social relations of production and on the relations between developed and developing countries (Dutt 1998, pp. 12–13; Todaro 1996, p. 82). Critics of FDI consider underdevelopment as an externally induced phenomenon. It is not original or traditional but is, in large part, the historical consequence of the relationship between developed and developing countries (Baran 1957; Frank 1969, p. 4).

More specifically, radical theorists like Dos Santos, Cardoso, Sunkel, Frank, Amin and Baran have argued that FDI arose in response to the need of northern industrial countries for new markets and/or new sources of cheap labour and other inputs (Baran 1957, pp. 177, 325; Frank 1966 and 1969; Cardoso 1972, pp. 91–2; Amin 1977, pp. 172–3; Helleiner 1989, pp. 1453–4). In their view, FDI is the "basis for a new type of technological industrial dependence to replace earlier forms of dependence" (Dos Santos 1970, p. 232).

Here FDI flows are seen as detrimental to socio-economic development. FDI flows have not supplemented but substituted for domestic savings, and have crowded out domestic entrepreneurs, worsening balance of payments problems in developing countries. The radical view also criticizes FDI flows for failing to address poverty in developing countries because FDI tends to introduce capital-intensive technology that creates less employment in relation to an expanding labour force, and establishes more exploitative employment conditions in developing countries (Baran 1957, pp. 177, 325; Frank 1966 and 1969; Cardoso 1972, pp. 91–2; Amin 1977, pp. 172–3; Helleiner 1989, pp. 1453–4).

While the debates on the impact of FDI on development are inconclusive, the empirical evidence seems to support the mainstream view in many cases. Several regression analyses have found that FDI has had a favourable impact on gross national investment, exports and above all, economic growth and poverty alleviation, especially in the cases of the Asian NICs. While the arguments and evidence in favour of FDI are compelling, the doubts raised by FDI's critics give us sufficient cause for concern and demand that FDI in practice and policy be carefully scrutinized if its harmful effects are to be diminished or negated.

Other factors, especially the role of government, may be vital. As will be discussed below, the success of Asian NICs compared to other developing countries in utilizing FDI to promote economic growth and alleviate poverty may be attributed to the role of government policies.

Government policy and FDI

The difference in impact and outcomes of FDI flows in East and Southeast Asian countries and other regions globally suggest that appropriate government policies can help to maximize this form of investment's positive effects. This section focuses on the role of governments in transitional economies in attracting and generally providing a favourable economic environment for FDI, especially under the framework of economic integration. In particular, this section examines investment incentives and trade policies.

Government intervention

There is increasing agreement that government policies do play an important role in ensuring and maximizing FDI's positive contributions to economic development. Such policies include:

- policies relating to resource allocation, innovation, education, trade, FDI competition;
- macroeconomic policies relating to fiscal, monetary, exchange rate management (Chen 1993, p.25; Clark and Chan 1994, 1995 cited in Bishop 1997, pp. 19–20; Dunning and Narula 1996, pp. 12–13; Narula 1996, p.17; Lecraw 1996, pp. 317–25).

In general, economic liberalization policies have the effect of inducing FDI flows to developing countries. Policies affecting the price and quality of natural resources and those aimed at improving the quality of human resources favourably affect the impact of FDI (Dunning and Narula 1996, pp. 19–20).

The evidence indicates that the volume as well as the positive impact of FDI will be maximized if a government creates a favourable economic environment and does not interfere directly in investment decisions and operations. However, the experiences of recently industrializing countries also show the need for selective government intervention to minimize the detrimental effects of FDI. The next section examines the relationship between FDI and government investment incentives and trade strategies especially during the transition towards a market economy.

Impact of investment incentives

Several developing countries have tried to attract FDI by providing generous incentives including tax reductions, rebates, concessions, investment allowances, low interest rates, cheap locations for factories, tariff protection and public subsidies (Hogendorn 1992, p. 421). Among these, tax incentives provide little or no inducement to FDI, compared to policies that directly lower investment costs, for three main reasons:

- tax holidays provide a "perverse" subsidy, providing little assistance when FIEs need it the most (that is, when FIEs make little or no profit) and providing assistance when FIEs do not need it (that is, when FIEs make a great deal of profit);
- their time limits discourage long-term foreign investors; and
- unlike cost-lowering incentives, tax holidays provide little attraction to risky investment as tax holidays accrue only when profits are made (Lim 1982, p. 208).

Several studies have shown that the major inducements to FDI tend to be a broad mix of economic variables (per capita income, balance of payments position, growth and inflation rates, low labour costs, the availability of raw materials, workforce skills, market size, and infrastructure); political factors as well as aid flows (Lall and Streeten 1977, pp. 36–8; Agodo 1978; Root and Ahmed 1979; Schneider and Frey 1985 cited in Helleiner 1989, p. 1450; Gold 1991, p. 22; Helleiner 1991, p. 148; Hogendorn 1992, p. 421; Lim 1994 cited in Bishop 1997, p. 13).

However, tax incentives can be effective in inducing FDI under specific circumstances. First, tax incentives may be important in the choice of location between competing countries with similar investment environments (Vernon 1977, p. 171; Lall and Streeten 1977, p. 38; Gold 1991; Bishop 1997, p. 17). Second, tax incentives may become an important determinant for export-oriented foreign investment decisions (Wells 1986; Gold 1991; Bishop 1997, pp. 16–17). The nature of production for export shows that export-oriented firms operate in highly competitive markets with slim margins and their costs are likely to be the major factor in determining profitability. Lower taxes will lower costs and increase profits (Wells 1986, p. 59). Moreover, export-oriented firms are highly mobile and sought-after as they generate job places. Hence those firms can, and do, move easily between countries to take advantage of tax incentives (World Bank 1997a, p. 17).

In conclusion, investment incentives—especially tax incentives—do not have much impact on the volume of general FDI received by developing countries. Such incentives seem to make a difference only when export-oriented firms are involved. This suggests that governments should use investment incentives selectively for attracting FDI intended to finance export-oriented activity.

Impact of government trade policies

Trade policies include import substitution industrialization (ISI), export oriented industrialization (EOI) and economic integration. This section examines the impact of trade policies on the effects of FDI and how economic integration helps to attract foreign investment.

Import substitution industrialization strategy

The major features of ISI are imposing tariffs and other restrictions, such as quotas and foreign exchange controls, on the import of selected consumer goods and promoting the development of local industries to meet domestic demand previously served by imported consumer goods. The major purpose of ISI is to develop indigenous industries, especially infant supportive industries, create employment to absorb rapidly increasing labour forces and alleviate poverty (Gillis et al. 1992, p. 441; Tan 1995, p. 61; Todaro 1996, p. 459).

The implementation of an ISI strategy at first provides strong impetus to promote economic growth and attract huge amounts of FDI. According to trade theory, trade restrictions will stimulate compensating factor flows. Trade protection creates local advantage, raising the cost of serving domestic markets through trade. In this case, trade protection will have inducing effects on foreign investors. When developing countries stop importing consumer goods, foreign exporters have to invest and produce locally to overcome protection barriers (McCulloch 1993, p. 43). While FDI induced by an ISI strategy contributes to initial high growth rates, such investment gradually has an unfavourable effect on socio-economic development for several reasons.

First, large FDI flows induced by ISI are a mere relocation of investment from developed to developing economies in response to the import restrictions of the former, not to the comparative advantages of the latter (Balasubramanyam and Salisu 1991, p. 193). As a consequence, such investment crowds out domestic entrepreneurs.

Second, FDI induced by ISI leads to a deterioration of the balance of payments position of the recipient country, creating a deficit in both current and capital accounts as a result of the excessive importation of capital equipment and intermediate products and the outflows of foreign exchange in the form of repatriated profits and royalties (Todaro 1996, p. 538; Calderon et al. 1996, pp. 258–9).

Third, foreign investors who invest behind tariff walls tend to apply out-of-date, inefficient technology (Gold 1991, p. 23; OECD 1998, p. 62).

Finally, FDI flows induced by ISI tend to adversely affect poverty alleviation; as ISI fails to provide a competitive environment, FDI flows tend to be capital intensive, less efficient and create few jobs in the host countries (Jenkins 1987, p. 73).

Export-oriented industrialization strategy

In contrast, an export-oriented industrialization (EOI) strategy tends to create a favourable environment which maximizes the positive impacts of FDI. An EOI strategy in developing countries is characterized by low or no trade barriers, and by the use of the comparative advantages of cheap labour and abundant raw materials for export-oriented production. This favourable environment is further boosted by market-determined exchange and interest rates and labour and goods prices in addition to minimal government intervention.[2] Such investment climates induce more FDI with efficient, labour-intensive techniques to developing countries, contributing to their socio-economic development with less negative effects for several reasons (Tan 1995, pp. 66–8; Todaro 1996).

First, FDI attracted by an EOI strategy tends to have fewer crowding-out effects on domestic entrepreneurs and in fact, this kind of FDI tends to supplement domestic investment and hence lead to an increase in gross national investment. Trade liberalization promotes high economic growth, less distortion in the investment environment and provides greater export opportunities that are essential for MNCs, especially when intra-firm trade is on the rise (Balasubramanyam and Salisu 1991, pp. 201–4; OECD 1998, p. 52).

Second, FDI induced by EOI tends to improve the balance of payments position by further increasing FDI flows and export earnings (Fry 1993 cited in OECD 1998, pp. 56–9; Tan 1995, pp. 34–5).

Third, an EOI strategy also improves technology transferred through FDI. When the choice of technology depends largely on the extent of competition, the international export market or non-distortion domestic market will force foreign investors to apply highly efficient, labour-intensive technology (Gillis et al. 1992, p. 389; World Bank 1997 cited in OECD 1998, p. 62).

Fourth, FDI flows induced by an export-oriented strategy have a favourable impact on economic growth. The opening of domestic markets and the competition of international markets force foreign investors to use resources efficiently (Chen 1990, p. 402, 1993, p. 56; Fry 1997, p. 530). Several studies have shown that FDI has led to high economic growth rates in East Asian countries that follow an EOI strategy but has led to increasing debt burdens in countries that still adopt an ISI strategy (Chen 1993, p. 56; Fry 1997, p. 530).

Finally, the implementation of an EOI strategy forces foreign investors to introduce labour-intensive technology and techniques, utilizing a largely cheap labour force in developing countries and creating more employment. This, in turn, helps to tackle the poverty problem (Helleiner 1975 cited in Chen 1990, p. 396; Wells 1993, p. 186).

Economic integration and FDI

Economic integration processes create static and dynamic gains that attract FDI flows. The static gains of economic integration are measured by trade creation between member countries of a free trade area or customs union by eliminating tariff and non-tariff barriers between member countries. The trade creation effects include a shift of production from high-cost to low-cost member countries in accordance with the comparative advantage of each member country (Root 1994, p. 254; Todaro 1996, pp. 482–5; Robson 1998, pp. 31–5). The dynamic gains of economic integration include the creation of a larger market and the achievement of economies of scale, research and development promotion, competition and improvement of terms of trade (Imada et al. 1991, p. 14).

Economic integration also creates trade diversion effects when a member country shifts from importing products from lowest-cost producers outside the trading bloc to importing them from other member countries as result of tariff removals within the trading bloc (Lawrence 1996, pp. 22–3).

There is a strong relationship between economic integration and FDI. An examination of the strategic responses of firms engaged in international production to each of the static and dynamic effects of economic integration process shows that there are likely to be four types of investment responses (Robson 1992, p. 104):

- *Defensive import-substituting investment* is MNCs' response to the trade diversion effects of economic integration. As tariff realignment generates locational advantages, MNCs move from exporting products

to the trading blocs to investing in production within trading blocs in order to maintain their market share.
- *Offensive import-substituting investment* is MNCs' investment to take advantage of growing demand and the opening up of new markets.
- *Reorganization investment* is a result of the trade-creation effects of integration, under which MNCs have to reallocate their economic activities in accordance with member countries' comparative advantages.
- *Rationalized investment* is FDI that responds to international differences in production costs generated by lowering production costs as a result of the reorganization of investment.

In general, it is argued that economic integration has induced FDI flows by creating larger markets and increasing production efficiency. On the other hand, the discriminatory removal of trade impediments has induced FDI to flow into trading blocs in order to avoid import tariffs and enjoy free access to member countries' markets. The formation of free trade areas like the ASEAN Free Trade Area, for example, will provide dynamic effects to enlarge the regional market, enable foreign investors to enjoy economies of scale and attract FDI flows toward making use of member countries' comparative advantages.

Government and FDI in transitional economies

The previous sections showed that appropriate government intervention through investment incentives, trade policy and infant industry protection contributes to attracting FDI. For transitional economies, appropriate government intervention appears to play a decisive role in attracting FDI flows: indirectly, by generating political, social and economic stability, or directly, by providing investment incentives and a favourable environment.

For transitional economies including those in Central and Eastern Europe, the former Soviet Union, China and Vietnam, FDI flows are considered important to the movement toward a market economy. FDI provides scarce investment capital, access to advanced technology and management techniques, as well as access to western markets. Moreover, FDI flows facilitate the privatization and restructuring process and promote the integration of those countries into the global economy (OECD 1995b, pp. 17–18; Dyker 1999, p. 9).

The inflow of FDI to these countries depend very much on the political, social and economic stability of those countries (Svetlicic et al. 1993, p. 8; Dunning 1993, p. 17; Tiusanen 1993, pp. 69–70). However, the role of government in maintaining stability and therefore attracting FDI flows in the countries in transition depends on the reform approach chosen by each country. Two distinctive reform approaches tend to predominate: the 'Big Bang' approach and the gradual approach.

The Big Bang approach[3] was introduced widely in Central and Eastern European countries and the countries of the former Soviet Union while the gradual approach has been followed by China since 1978. In China, liberalization policies began first in selected areas and were then applied more extensively. In fact, the reforms in China went through several stages of "combining plan with market" (World Bank 1996, p. 10).

The role of the government under each reform approach also differs substantially. In a planned economy, the government controls almost every socio-economic activity. Under the Big Bang approach, the role of government is reduced almost overnight to controlling only a minimum of economic activities such as defence or major public goods. In contrast, under the gradual approach, government intervention is reduced through several phases until the necessary institutions of a market economy have fully emerged (World Bank 1996; Pomfret 1996).

These different reform approaches in countries in transition have generated divergent results. The Central and Eastern European countries that followed the Big Bang approach all suffered economic slowdowns and high inflation over the 1989–95 period. In contrast, China has experienced substantial economic growth and improvement in social indicators. China has achieved a high GDP growth rate of 9.4 percent over the 1989–95 period, while life expectancy has increased by 2.1 percent and infant mortality reduced by 11.1 percent.

The success of the gradual approach in China and the failure of the Big Bang approach in Central and Eastern European countries, especially in Russia, are attributable to several factors such as the social and economic structure of each country, and the existing conditions before reform (World Bank 1996). Appropriate government intervention has also played a decisive role during the transition period in those countries. In the case of Russia, the lack of appropriate government intervention, the sudden disappearance of planning institutions, and the slow development of new market institutions led to the failure of the co-ordination system for the whole economy (World Bank 1996, p. 27).

Reforms in China, unlike those of Russia, have been kept under close government control. The reforms were first carried out on an experimental basis and gradually expanded to the whole country (Spulber 1997, p. 129). This government control has served as a "co-ordinating function, limiting disruptions to the production and trade during the phased building up of market institutions" (World Bank 1996, p. 25).

Such a smooth and stable environment, in turn, allows China to achieve high economic growth, improve living standards and creates a favourable environment for FDI.

The combination of an open door policy, political, social and economic stability, as well as a high level of economic growth, also attracts FDI to countries in transition (Svetlicic et al. 1993, p. 8; Dunning 1993, p. 17; Tiusanen 1993, pp. 69–70). It has been emphasized that "what investors need is an assurance that the goal-posts will not be moved during the lifetime of their commercial undertakings" (Svetlicic et al. 1993, p. 8). Besides the indirect effect in attracting FDI by generating stable social, political and economic conditions, the government in countries in transition can also directly provide a favourable environment for FDI. Dunning (1993) states that the potential of countries in transition to attract and make use of FDI flows will depend on the government's success in:

> ...reshaping of attitudes to work and wealth creation, the redesigning of the business and legal framework, especially with respect to property rights and contractual relationships, the costs of setting up a market system, and the introduction of macro-economic policies which encourage domestic savings, but accept the discipline of currency convertibility and an open trading system (Dunning 1993, p. 20).

The experience of FDI flows in countries in transition seems to support arguments about the important role of government. For instance, FDI for China in 1996, where the government still plays an important role in socio-economic activities, was more than 16 times that of Russia, where government control and co-ordination is kept to a minimum (Meyer 1998, p. 30).

The low level of FDI flows in Russia are due to political, social and economic instability and a lack of appropriate government intervention (Adjubei 1993, p. 100; Popov 1998, p. 122; Barz 1999, p. 111). The key problems faced by foreign investors in Russia are "the permanent state of flux of the legal framework and the discrepancies between enactment and enforcement" (Barz 1999, p. 111). Such problems, caused by the sudden reduction of government intervention at the early stage of transition, have left a vacuum and many central, regional and local authorities have competed to fill this vacuum. Such competition has produced a "striking opaqueness and inconsistency" in the legal framework that governs the operation of FDI flows (Barz 1999, p. 111).

In conclusion, government intervention during transitions has played a decisive role in attracting FDI flows through maintaining political, social and economic stability and providing investment incentives and a favourable environment for FDI. The experiences of FDI in China and Russia show that the conditions of countries in transition towards a market economy require appropriate government intervention. Such government intervention will work hand in hand with market institutions that are being established during the transition in order to create a favourable environment for FDI.

Conclusion

This chapter has examined several theories, in particular, the mainstream and radical views about the motivation for, and the impact of, FDI on socio-economic development. The development experiences of East Asian countries and countries in transition towards a market economy have shown that government policies can help to maximize the positive impacts and minimize the detrimental effects of FDI flows and economic integration. However, there are still some questions, especially for countries in transition:

- What are the effects, either useful or detrimental, of FDI flows on socio-economic development during the transition from a highly planned towards a market-oriented economy?
- What should governments do during such a transition period to maximize the positive and minimize the detrimental effects of FDI flows?

These questions will be addressed in the following chapters by analyzing the impact of FDI in Vietnam between 1988 and 1998 as well as by examining the policies of the government of Vietnam with regards to FDI.

Notes

[1] The impacts of FDI flows on economic growth have been calculated by using the Harrod-Domar model. If the output is called Y, then:

$$Y = K / k$$
$$\Delta Y/Y = \Delta K/(kY) = I/(kY) = \frac{(S/Y + F/Y)}{k}$$

or $\quad g = s/k$
Where $\quad$ K: Capital stock
k: Capital-output ratio (or Incremental Capital Output ratio – ICOR)
DY: Change in output
DK: Change in capital stock = I: Gross investment
s: Saving rate
g: Growth rate
S: Gross domestic savings
F: Foreign capital

[2] There are inconclusive debates on the role of government intervention under EOI strategy, especially in the case of Asian NICs, where government played an active role in promoting EOI strategy.

[3] According to the World Bank, the Big Bang (or all-out) approach includes:
- rapid price and trade liberalization with a determined stabilization programme to restore or maintain price stability;
- quick moves to current account convertibility;
- opening of market to entry by new private businesses; and
- starting several other reforms such as privatization, financial sector reform, and tax reform (World Bank 1996, p. 9).

3
Socio-Economic Reforms and FDI in Vietnam

The success of East and Southeast Asian countries in utilizing FDI flows to promote socio-economic development suggests that appropriate government policies can help to maximize the positive impact of FDI while minimizing any detrimental effects. This significant role of government in influencing the overall impact of FDI on an economy seems to be borne out in the case of Vietnam. This chapter first briefly reviews the socio-economic reforms in Vietnam which started in 1986 and were the foundation for foreign direct investment into that country. This is followed by an examination of the magnitude and trends in FDI since 1988.

Overview of socio-economic development

With a population of 78 million (GSO 1999b) and a GDP per capita of $352 (in 1998), Vietnam is still one of the poorest countries in the world (World Bank 1999b, UN 1999). However, in terms of social development, Vietnam has achieved outstanding results compared to other low income countries. Social indicators such as literacy, life expectancy and infant mortality rates for Vietnam are comparable to those in lower middle income countries such as Malaysia or Indonesia (UN 1999).

From unification in 1975 up until 1986, the economy of Vietnam was characterized as a highly concentrated planned economy in which the state played a dominant role. The private sector and FDI were not encouraged. External economic relations were mainly with the socialist countries of Eastern Europe, especially the former Soviet Union. Under such a planned system economic system and unfavourable international conditions, the economy suffered several difficulties. Gross Domestic Product (GDP) growth was low and agricultural output was insufficient to meet domestic demand, while inflation remained at over 700 percent in 1986, as shown in Table 3.1.

Table 3.1 Major Indicators of Macroeconomic Performance of the Vietnamese Economy, 1986–98

	1986	1987	1988	1989	1990	1991	1992	1993	1994	1995	1996	1997	1998	1999	2000	2001
GDP growth rate (%)	0.3	3.7	5.9	8.0	5.1	6.0	8.6	8.1	8.8	9.5	9.3	8.2	5.8	4.8	6.8	6.8
GDP per capita ($)	n.a.	n.a.	n.a.	n.a.	n.a.	n.a.	156.0	n.a.	217.0	n.a.	19.0	n.a.	352.0	n.a.	400.0	n.a.
Export growth (%)	23.5	20.2	80.1	31.1	18.0	21.2	20.6	35.8	28.2	41.0	24.8	2.4	23.2	25.2	4.0	n.a.
Import growth (%)	5.6	19.3	18.3	6.3	18.7	20.3	39.3	48.6	43.7	39.0	-0.2	-1.1	1.1	34.5	2.3	n.a.
Inflation rate (%)	775.0	232.0	394.0	28.0	67.5	67.6	17.6	5.2	14.4	12.7	4.5	3.6	9.2	0.1	-0.5	0.8

Source: World Bank 1995a, 1995b, 1996, 1999, 2002; GSO 1996, 1999b; United Nations 1999.

From 1986, the government of Vietnam started its reform programme (*Doi Moi*), moving from a highly concentrated planning mechanism towards a market-oriented economy. Accompanying the movement towards a market-oriented economy, Vietnam also implemented an open door policy, promoting external economic co-operation with all countries, encouraging foreign trade and investment. Socio-economic reform has turned Vietnam into a "multi-sectoral economy in accordance with the market based on state management and Socialist orientation" (Reinhardt 1993, p. 71). The main aims of these reforms in Vietnam are to:

- achieve sustainable economic growth in order to deepen macroeconomic reforms, alleviate poverty and foster industrialization;
- maintain political, social and economic stability;
- guarantee equity and equal opportunity for all; and
- create a people-centred development process that is implemented by the people, for the people (United Nations 1999, p. 1).

To achieve such objectives, several sectoral reforms have been carried out (Than and Tan 1993; Fforde and de Vylder 1996; Harvie and Tran 1997). In the agricultural sector, farming co-operatives have been replaced by farm households and long-term land use rights have been given to farmers in order to stabilize and increase agricultural output.

In the industrial sector, more autonomy has been given to state-owned enterprises (SOEs) and the system of government subsidies for SOEs was abolished. All SOEs have been put on self-financing bases and they have been made responsible for their own production, marketing and profits. The government also shifted the focus of investment from heavy toward light and export-oriented industries. The private sector has been encouraged and promoted.

In the financial sector, the government has limited its control to the price of a few strategic commodities and allowed the free market to determine the prices of the majority of commodities. In the trade sector, the decentralization and liberalization process has been carried out intensively. The government no longer controls trade by command or plan but uses market tools such as taxes, quotas and tariffs and FDI has been promoted. At the end of 1987, the government of Vietnam promulgated the *Law on Foreign Investment* to attract foreign capital and technology to support the socio-economic development.

As the result of those reforms, the country has achieved encouraging initial results. Table 3.1 shows that from 1987 up to 1997, the economy achieved high annual growth rates of around 8 percent, while export and import growth remained at high levels. Industrial and agricultural production also grew rapidly and Vietnam moved from being a rice importer before 1986 to become the world's third largest rice exporter in the early 1990s. Inflation was reduced and has remained at single digits since 1996. As the result of high economic growth, the poverty alleviation process has achieved striking results. The proportion of people classified as poor fell from 53 percent in 1993 to 37 percent in 1998 (GOV and World Bank 1999, p. ii). Successful economic growth in Vietnam since 1986 has been attributed to the government's socio-economic reform policy. Foreign direct investment flows, one of the major elements of these reforms, have been argued to be one of the key factors in Vietnam's successful economic development.

Volume and forms of FDI in Vietnam

Foreign direct investment started to trickle into Vietnam in 1977, when the country introduced its first Foreign Investment Rules to attract capital to develop the country after the long period of war. However, due to unfavourable international conditions, the 1977 Rules did not bring in substantial amounts of FDI.

As one of the major elements of the 1986 socio-economic reform, FDI was actively promoted by Vietnam's government through the promulgation of the Law on Foreign Investment in late 1987. The 1987 Law contains "the government's guidelines, the Socialist orientations, with the purpose of strengthening national interests and meeting the need and interests of foreign investors" (Luu 1997, p. 89). The 1987 Law has been considered as "one of the most liberal in Southeast Asia", more comprehensive and liberal than that of China (*Economist* 1987; Gates and Truong 1994, p. 14). The Law provides conditions favourable to FDI by offering generous tax incentives, import privileges and by not imposing a minimum capital requirement.

Vietnam's laws and regulations relating to FDI have been liberalized gradually to provide a more favourable foreign investment environment, and to broaden the rights of both Vietnamese and foreign investors. The Law on Foreign Investment in Vietnam has been amended twice, in 1990 and 1992, and renewed twice, in 1996 and 2000. The success of the Law on Foreign Investment in Vietnam has been reflected in the large inflows of FDI to Vietnam since 1988 as shown in Table 3.2. This has been despite the US trade embargo on Vietnam which was not lifted until 1994.

Between 1988 and 1998, about $35,302 million of FDI was committed for investment in 2,588 projects in several sectors. However, 464 projects

Table 3.2 Overview of Foreign Direct Investment Flows in Vietnam, 1988–98

	1988–90	1991	1992	1993	1994	1995	1996	1997	1998
Number of projects	211	152	195	273	371	412	368	331	275
Committed capital ($ m)	1,582	1,294	2,036	2,652	4,071	6,616	8,640	4,514	3,897
Number of cancelled projects	6	37	48	34	58	57	52	77	95
Investment capital of cancelled projects ($m)	24	293	402	79	217	477	1,035	334	2,433
Number of projects with increased investment capital	1	6	10	51	73	122	134	143	133
Increased investment capital ($m)	0.3	7.7	49	222	504	1,247	684	1,095	770
Actual committed capital ($m)	1,558.3	1,008.7	1,683	2,795	4,358	7,386	8,289	5,275	2,234
Growth rate of actual committed capital (%)	n.a.	64.7	166.8	166.1	155.9	169.5	112.2	63.6	42.4
Legal capital ($m)	1,332	680	1,406	1,526	1,796	2,805	3,012	2,115	1,795
of which Vietnam's contribution ($m)	161	156	185	311	463	723	692	327	626
Average size of project ($m)	7.6	8.8	11.4	11.7	13.9	20.8	26.2	20.8	12.4
Number of finished projects	2	1	3	3	1	2	3	3	3
Investment capital of finished project ($m)	0.26	1	13.94	15.51	0.13	0.5	74.56	0.82	19.1
FDI implementation ($m)	262.5	213	394	1,099	1,946	2,671	2,646	3,250	1,956
Growth rate of implemented capital (%)	n.a.	n.a.	185.0	278.9	177.1	137.3	99.1	122.8	60.2
Ratio of FDI implementation over actual commitment (%)	0	21.1	23.4	39.3	44.7	36.2	31.9	61.6	87.6

Source: Mekong Project Development Facility (MPDF) 1999a, 1999b; Ha Thang 2000 and various World Bank Country Reports.

with a total investment capital of $5,294 million were cancelled, while $4,579 million of investment capital was increased for existing projects over the same period. As a result, the actual committed FDI flows in Vietnam over this period totalled $34,587 million for 2,124 projects. There was a particularly impressive growth rate of around 65 percent of committed FDI between 1991–95. FDI implementation also increased rapidly, especially between 1991 and 1997, up from $213 million in 1991 to $3,250 million in 1997 but then reduced to $1,520 million in 1999. The ratio of implementation over commitment also rose from 1988, increasing from 21.1 percent in 1991 to 87.6 percent in 1998 and for the whole period from 1988 to 1998, $14.2 billion of FDI has been realized, accounting for 41 percent of total committed FDI. The implementation of committed FDI in Vietnam seems to be better compared to China, where the same ratio for the period 1979–96 was only 37.3 percent (Zhang 1999, p. 12). In 1996, Vietnam was the world's second largest recipient of FDI, calculated as a percentage of its GNP (World Bank 1997a, p. 17).

The average size of FDI projects also increased from $7.6 million in 1988–90 to $26.2 million in 1996 before reducing to $12.4 million in 1998. For the whole period 1988–98, the average size of FDI projects was $16.3 million, some $2–3 million higher than that of China (VEN 1998). Moreover, several existing projects requested an increase in their investment capital, adding to total FDI commitment of over $4.5 billion over the 1988–98 period. In 1995, for example, this additional investment capital was $1,247 million, accounting for 16.9 percent of total FDI committed in that year.

On the other hand, a number of projects were cancelled for various reasons, but mainly due to difficulties in mobilizing investment capital and other difficulties associated with the regional financial crisis. The number of cancelled projects and their investment capital increased since 1996 and reached $2.4 billion in 1998. Of the cancelled projects, the majority had been approved during the 1988–92 period when the economy of Vietnam was still undergoing significant reform toward a market-oriented economy and the knowledge of foreign investors about Vietnam's market was still limited.

Table 3.3 reveals that since 1991, joint ventures have been the dominant form of FDI flows in Vietnam, in terms of both commitment and implementation. In 1994, the amended Law on Foreign Investment allowed a new category of operation, Build-Operation-Transfer (BOT) to be implemented in Vietnam, and its share in FDI flows has increased since then. The 100 percent foreign-owned form also has been increasing in response to changes in government policy. Another form of FDI flows, the Business Co-operation Contract (BCC), which played an important

Table 3.3 Foreign Direct Investment Commitment and Implementation by Forms of Investment, 1988–98 (percent)

	1988–90	1991		1992		1993		1994		1995		1996		1997		1998	
	Com.	Com.	Impl.	Com.	Impl.	Com.	Impl.	Com.	Impl.	Com.	Impl.	Com.	Impl.	Com.	Impl.	Com.	Impl.
Joint ventures	36.7	60.6	61.9	56.3	45.9	66.9	47.2	74.1	51.2	69.1	51.7	76.7	58.4	50.2	64.5	57.3	34.8
– with SOEs	n.a.	59.8	59.5	55.6	44.3	65.8	45.9	71.8	49.6	67.2	50.7	75.1	57.2	47.5	59.2	52.2	33.8
– with private sector	n.a.	0.9	1.8	0.7	1.6	1.1	1.3	2.3	1.5	1.9	1.1	1.6	1.2	2.6	2.4	5.0	1.0
Business co-operation contract	60.1	28.3	36.3	25.1	29.1	4.7	32.8	3.5	32.8	5.4	29.8	1.2	13.4	17.8	2.3	17.5	54.4
Build-operation-transfer	0.0	0.0	0.0	0.0	0.0	0.0	0.0	0.0	0.0	0.5	0.2	7.2	0.0	5.1	0.1	0.0	0.4
100% Foreign-owned	3.1	11.1	1.8	18.6	25.3	28.5	20.2	22.5	16.1	25.0	18.3	14.9	28.2	26.9	33.2	25.3	10.5

Com.: Commitment
Imp.: Implemented
Source: Mekong Project Development Facility (MPDF) 1999a, 1999b

role in the early years, decreased to less than 6 percent of total FDI commitment in the 1993–96 period.

Vietnam's major domestic participants in all forms of FDI (with the exception of 100 percent foreign-owned ventures) have been SOEs, while participation from the private sector has been small both in terms of the number of projects and committed capital. For the whole period 1988–98, Vietnam's private sector has been involved in around only 7.8 percent of the number of projects and less than 2 percent of committed FDI. The reasons for the vast gaps between private and state sector involvement in FDI projects will be discussed in the following chapter.

The sectoral distribution of FDI in Vietnam between 1988 and 1998 shows that both committed and implemented FDI have increased in manufacturing industries and food industries but decreased in hotels and tourism, and apartments and office building. For the 1988–98 period, the manufacturing and service sectors became dominant for both FDI commitment and implementation, while the primary sector, which played a key role during the 1988–90 period, decreased in importance.

The small share of FDI flows to the agricultural sector has been another cause for concern. The agricultural sector is a significant part of Vietnam's economy, accounting for over 24 percent of GDP and 68.8 percent of the labour force in 1997, but it received only a small amount of FDI flows of around $1.9 billion, or less than 5.8 percent of the total FDI, over the 1988–98 period. This amount also includes several projects in the manufacturing industries such as food processing, wood processing and animal feed production. If those FDI projects are excluded, the total amount of FDI in cultivation, animal husbandry, afforestation and other husbandry agricultural activities can be said to have fallen to $462.1 million or 1.5 percent of total FDI flows over the 1988–98 period (MPDF 1999a, 1999b). Compared with the total domestic investment in agriculture (including public and local private investment) over the same period, FDI flows have been small. The public investment fund in the agriculture sector in 1996 and 1997, for example, was $573 million, $110 million higher than the FDI to the agricultural sector for the whole period under review. Hence the small amounts of FDI flows to agriculture did not create any significant impacts on the growth of this sector.

Foreign direct investment flows into Vietnam from over 60 countries and territories in the world, including developing countries, developed countries and Newly Industrializing Countries (NICs). Table 3.4 shows the FDI flows to Vietnam from the top 10 foreign countries in terms

Table 3.4 Top 10 Countries Classified by Foreign Direct Investment Commitment, 1988–98

Rank	Country	Committed FDI ($ million)	Share in total (percent)
1	Singapore	5,713.1	16.1
2	Taiwan	4,415.9	12.4
3	Hongkong	3,570.9	10.0
4	Japan	3,299.1	9.3
5	South Korea	2,973.7	8.4
6	France	1,832.8	5.2
7	British Virgin Islands	1,710.7	4.8
8	Russian Federation	1,498.4	4.2
9	United States	1,189.7	3.3
10	United Kingdom	1,160.7	3.2

Source: GSO 1999b, pp. 249–50.

of FDI commitment. While Asian NICs have been leading foreign investors in Vietnam, FDI from developed countries of EC and North America have become increasingly important.

Stages of foreign direct investment in Vietnam

Foreign direct investment flows into Vietnam can be divided into four stages.

Early stage, 1988–90

During the early stage, FDI flows focused solely on oil and gas sector and hotels and tourism and other service industries which accounted for 91.1 percent of the total FDI commitment. The FDI flows into the manufacturing sector, however, accounted for only 8.9 percent because foreign investors were not familiar with Vietnam's market and investment regulations.

The projects committed during the early stage, except for the oil and gas industry, were small, short term and aimed for quick returns. Business co-operation contracts were the dominant FDI form as the majority of FDI flows were in the telecommunication and oil and gas industries where only joint ventures and BCCs were allowed.

The take-off stage, 1991–94

During this stage, annual FDI commitment increased significantly from $1 billion in 1991 to $3.85 billion in 1994 while annual FDI implementation increased more than nine times to $1.95 billion in 1994. At this stage, FDI flows from Asian countries, especially ASEAN and Asian NICs, increased rapidly. The manufacturing and service sectors became important as foreign investors became more familiar with Vietnam's market and started looking for long-term business in Vietnam by establishing joint ventures with local partners. By 1994, joint ventures accounted for 74.1 percent of total FDI commitment while BCC fell to only 3.5 percent.

The consolidation stage, 1995–96

This stage was marked by the lifting of the U.S. trade embargo against Vietnam and as a result, more FDI flows, especially from the United States and Japan, were registered. In 1995, FDI flows from Japan increased to $1.35 billion compared to $227 million in 1994 while FDI flows from North America increased by almost five times. In 1996, Vietnam achieved a record $8.3 billion of FDI commitment. The manufacturing and service sectors were still major components of FDI commitment, while the primary sector accounted for only 2.1 percent of total FDI commitment.

The fourth stage 1997–98

This stage was associated with the regional financial crisis and marked by a sharp decline in FDI flows. In 1998, newly committed FDI was as low as $1.46 billion, a decline from $4.18 billion in 1997. This was a direct consequence of the financial crisis that affected almost all East Asian NICs and ASEAN countries, the major foreign investors in Vietnam. For example, the FDI commitment from ASEAN countries in 1998 was only $8.06 million compared to the 1996 commitment of $3.45 billion. Moreover, the devaluation of several local currencies as a direct consequence of the regional economic downturn also reduced the comparative advantage of Vietnam's cheap labour and hence reduced its attractiveness to foreign investors. Foreign investment in the form of 100 percent foreign owned enterprises also increased to over 25 percent of total FDI commitment during this stage, due to factors that will be examined later.

In conclusion, flows of FDI to Vietnam since 1988 increased significantly, moving from a focus on the primary sector (especially oil and gas industries) toward concentrating on manufacturing and services. That trend of FDI flows may place Vietnam in the end of stage one or the early part of stage two of Dunning's five stages of the investment development path, where inward direct investment starts to rise while outward investment is still low.

Underlying factors

The FDI flows to Vietnam, especially the huge amount of investment after 1990 as well as its significant decline after 1996, have been attributed to several factors. According to Dunning's eclectic theory, such factors can be classified into three groups: locational advantages, ownership advantages and internalization factors (Dunning and Narula 1996, pp. 1–2).

Locational advantages

The locational advantages refer to the natural, geographical and socio-economic conditions of Vietnam that attract FDI flows. The strategic location of Vietnam in Southeast Asia, the most rapidly growing region in the world during much of the 1950–97 period, allows Vietnam to take part in a dynamic economic growth process, and makes it more attractive to foreign investors. The proximity between Vietnam and other Asian NICs and ASEAN countries also attracts FDI flows from those countries to Vietnam.

Vietnam's political and economic stability is another advantage. Since 1986, the economy of Vietnam has stabilized and grown rapidly at around 8 percent per annum. Exports and imports have also increased significantly while inflation has remained in single digits (Table 3.1). Several foreign investors have chosen Vietnam instead of other, similarly endowed, developing countries in Africa or Latin America because of this stability.

Vietnam's wide range of natural mineral resources also attracted foreign investors, especially during the early stages. There are large unexploited deposits of coal, wolfram, lead, zinc, bauxite and iron located in the North and Central parts of the country while promising large reserves of oil and gas are located offshore of Vietnam as well as in the Mekong and Red River deltas. Since 1988, several oil companies have been working on the exploration of those fields.

Another advantage of Vietnam that attracts FDI is its abundant and cheap but relatively well-educated labour force. The total labour force of Vietnam in 1997 was 37 million or 47.7 percent of the total population. The labour force increases rapidly at an annual growth rate of 3.5 percent or 1.2 million people and this makes Vietnam's labour force rather young (GSO 1999b, p. 10). It is projected that, by the year 2005, people aged between 20 and 30 years will account for 37 percent of the total labour force (GSO 1994, p. 75). Moreover, about 24.8 million people (or 67.1 percent of the labour force) are now working in the agricultural sector. This creates a large potential labour pool to meet the increasing demand for labour for foreign invested enterprises (FIEs). On the other hand, because Vietnam has maintained its high literacy rate of 89 percent in 1997–98, its labour force is also well-educated (UNDP 1999). The 1989 population census revealed that over 3 million of the total labour force of 29 million had obtained at least some technical training qualification.

Looking for cheap labour has been the main motivation of several foreign investors coming to Vietnam. Vietnam's labour costs have remained lower than those of other countries in the region. The wage levels in Vietnam in 1996 remained the lowest for all categories of labour (Table 3.5). Even after other countries in the region had significantly depreciated their currencies against the US dollar as a consequence of the regional financial crisis, Vietnam maintained its comparative advantage of cheap labour.

Table 3.5 Vietnam's Average Wage Levels, 1996 ($/day)

Country	Minimum Wage Unskilled labour	Unskilled labour	Skilled labour	Technicians	Engineers	Middle Managers
Indonesia	0.70–2.85	2.00–3.00	6.10	250	380	560
Malaysia	None	7.97	13.28	578	1,395	1,992
Philippines	4.19–5.65	4.00–6.70	7.00–9.17	350–550	650–962	1,076–1,307
Taiwan	28.50		37.5	51.5	1,378	1,568	2,225
Thailand	5.07–6.25	5.12–6.13	6.61–7.28	282–560	584–749	700–1,221
Vietnam	0.78	1.29–1.37	2.15–2.38	100–185	195	220

Source: Table 1.3 in World Bank 1998, p. 7.

Furthermore, as labour costs have risen dramatically in several developed countries, there has been a need for MNCs to invest overseas to secure lower labour costs and hence reduce production costs. Table 3.5 shows that labour costs in Taiwan, for instance, are 10 to 40 times higher than in Vietnam. A survey of Japanese corporations operating overseas in 1996 revealed that 60.4 percent of Japanese corporations investing in Vietnam have done so to secure low-cost labour (Table 3.6) (Masuyama and Tamao 1998, p. 70).

The large and fast developing domestic market is another factor that attracts FDI to Vietnam. With a population of around 78 million in 1998 growing at an annual rate of 1.7 percent, and an economy that grows at a high annual rate of around 8 percent, Vietnam is an important market for several kinds of manufactured products and services. Table 3.6 shows that 86.4 percent of responding Japan corporations investing in Vietnam were cultivating new markets (63.5 percent) or expanding existing markets (22.9 percent).

Table 3.6 Japanese Corporations' Reasons for Investing Overseas (percentage of responding corporations)

	Vietnam	Malaysia	Thailand	Indonesia	Philippines	Myanmar	China
Expansion of existing local market	22.9	46.5	55.6	58.1	44.4	17.6	49.2
Cultivating new market	63.5	22.5	35.7	33.6	28.9	58.8	58.3
Export to Japan	28.1	22.5	27.0	29.4	33.3	23.5	30.8
Export to third country	30.2	38.0	31.7	35.3	44.4	35.3	27.9
Diversifying production	29.2	33.8	33.3	31.9	40.0	35.3	29.6
Securing low cost labour	60.4	31.0	32.5	44.5	57.8	76.5	47.9
Component supply to assembly manufacturers	14.6	23.9	34.1	24.4	33.3	11.8	18.3
Avoiding exchange risk	5.2	11.3	9.5	6.7	11.1	5.9	6.7

Source: Japan Export-Import Bank 1996 in Masuyama and Tamao 1998, p. 70.

In addition to securing Vietnam's domestic market, several foreign investors consider Vietnam as a suitable place in which to produce export products for neighbouring countries and overseas markets such as Laos, Cambodia, Southern China, the European Community (EC) or North America. Vietnam signed a trade agreement with the European Community in 1992, it joined ASEAN in 1995, and APEC in 1999, signed a trade agreement with the United States in July 2000, and is actively negotiating to join the World Trade Organization (WTO). As a result, foreign investors may expect to get access to the lucrative markets of North America, the European Community or ASEAN and other neighbouring countries. The trade agreement signed with the European Community on textiles and garments, for example, has given Vietnam's textile and garment industries access to a market of 350 million people and the quota for Vietnam's garments to the European Community has increased from $250 million in 1993 to $450 million in 1997 and is expected to reach $600–$650 million per annum in the 1998–2000 period (Nguyen 1999a).

The last, very important factor, that attracts FDI flows to Vietnam is the government's positive attitude. This is reflected in Vietnam's Prime Minister's statement that:

> All foreign businesses of various forms, including the 100 percent foreign-invested enterprises, are an integral part of the Vietnamese economy. That means Vietnam's interest is closely attached to that of foreign investors. If you are successful, the Vietnamese economy will develop. Otherwise, when you face difficulties or loss, we will partly suffer (STM 1998).

The stance toward FDI has also been seen in several changes, renewals and amendments regarding the Law on Foreign Investment as well as related regulations and circulars. Such changes and amendments aim to remove the obstacles against FDI or to improve the investment environment in Vietnam such as providing more tax incentives, reducing the charges for land, power and water supplies or simplifying investment procedures. The government also established a favourable legal environment for FDI flows by signing an agreement on the promotion and protection of investment with approximately 30 countries, and participating in the Washington agreement to resolve the conflict between government and foreign investors.

While several Western researchers argue that the government of Vietnam has not done enough to improve the environment for FDI, and that government intervention should be further reduced to a minimum (World Bank 1999b; IMF 1999; Dixon 2000), such arguments seem not to suit the real conditions of Vietnam during its transition towards a market-oriented economy. In fact, within the 10 years from 1988 to 1998, the government of Vietnam set up, almost from nothing, a legal system that promotes a multi-sector economy. Moreover, the gradual approach adopted by the government of Vietnam has contributed to the maintenance of social and economic stability and created a favourable environment for all economic activities, including FDI. The World Bank praised the success of Vietnam's gradual reform in its 1996 *World Development Report* (World Bank 1996). The reality in Vietnam has shown that government intervention over the transition period from 1986 has generated the necessary conditions to achieve social and economic stability, to mobilize domestic sources and foreign sources, including FDI, to achieve sustainable development. The Big Bang approach, as suggested by many Western critics, would have done more harm than good for Vietnam as it has done for many Central and Eastern European countries.

Ownership advantages

Another factor that explains the large FDI flows to Vietnam is the ownership advantages of foreign investors who invest in Vietnam. The ability of MNCs, their technological capabilities, managerial and marketing skills as well as their access to key parts and the financial market give them special advantages as foreign investors in Vietnam. After several years of applying planning mechanisms, Vietnam's enterprises are in desperate need of foreign capital, technologies and management skills as well as access to international markets and financial sources.

Internalization factors

The last set of factors that attracts FDI flows to Vietnam is internalization factors, chiefly government taxes, tariffs and other policies designed to protect the domestic market and infant industries. As the government industrialization policies are to promote several essential infant industries, several financial incentives, high import tariffs and non-tariff barriers have been used to promote domestic production and protect local infant industries. Vietnam's programme to implement the ASEAN Free Trade Area (AFTA) includes the reduction of tax to 5 percent by the year 2003 for only 1,661 groups of goods and accounts for only 51.6 percent of total groups of goods in Vietnam's import tax schedule (MOF 1998). The exclusion list, the temporary exclusion list and the agricultural-sensitive list consist of 1,556 groups of goods with higher import tax of 20 percent or over (MOF 1998). Moreover, several other non-tariff barriers such as export–import quotas and licences have also been used to protect the domestic market. All these trade related measures have had a significant impact: since the early 1990s, the government's industrialization policy, high import taxes and non-tariff barriers have attracted large amounts of FDI.

Obstacles to foreign direct investment

While locational and ownership advantages and internalization factors explain the growth in FDI flows to Vietnam during the 1988–96 period, there are several factors that explain the subsequent decline of FDI since 1997. Those factors are the Asian regional economic crisis, poor infrastructure, the high costs of operation and an inefficient bureaucracy.

The Asian regional economic slowdown has had several detrimental impacts on the economy of Vietnam and on the performance of FIEs in particular. As East Asian countries accounted for about 70 percent of the FDI and over 75 percent of the export market of Vietnam, the financial crisis in those countries has led to the reduction of around 12 percent of Vietnam's GDP (WB 1998, p. 4 and p. 14). The regional economic crisis created financial difficulties for many foreign investors in Vietnam, and a reduction in the demand for exports from Vietnam. In terms of FDI flows, the regional crisis has put several FDI projects on hold and either stopped or slowed down implementation. The implemented FDI in 1998 reduced by 40 percent compared to 1997. The sector which suffered the most was property development.

While the Asian regional economic crisis had a negative effect on FDI projects since 1996, poor physical and economic infrastructures also generated obstacles for FDI projects since the first days of operation. Poor transport systems, scarce or costly power and water supply systems are the major reasons that led to increasing operating costs for FIEs in Vietnam. In addition, an underdeveloped banking and financial system also created many difficulties in terms of the financing and operation of projects (Le 1997, pp. 84–5; Nestor 1997, p. 168; Harvie and Tran 1997, p. 76).

Other factors that have contributed to the delay in implementation of many FDI projects are land clearance and resettlement. Many projects have faced lengthy delays in obtaining land use rights[1], as well as in negotiating on removal compensation and resettlement (Masuyama and Tamao 1998, p. 76).

The lack of a long-term strategy for FDI flows from the beginning has led to the problem of oversupply in some industries of which the hotel and automobile industries are typical examples. The idle capacity of the hotel industry was 65 percent while that of the automobile industry was 80 percent in 1998 (MPI 1998).

The last problem that hinders the FDI flows and performance in Vietnam is the implementation of the Law on Foreign Investment. Notwithstanding the government's positive efforts, the implementation of the Law and Vietnam's bureaucracy has been a stumbling block for foreign investors. Such problems were less worrying to foreign investors in the early stages but have proved to be very serious recently, especially in the circumstances of the Asian regional economic crisis. First, there is a lack of clarity in the regulations regarding FDI flows. While the Law on Foreign Investment of Vietnam was considered liberal and several attempts have been made to amend and improve it, there are several issues which remain unclear. Such problems lead to differences in interpreting the Law and regulations between several agencies and organizations and this confuses foreign investors. This problem occurs in several aspects of the FDI process, especially in implementing investment incentives and the land clearance and resettlement process (i.e. tax deduction, land price adjustment) (Okada 1996, pp. 61–2; Nguyen 1997, pp. 11–24).

Second, there are cumbersome administrative procedures involved in appraising and managing FDI projects. The government has attempted to streamline this process by decentralizing the issuing of investment licences, and allowing provincial authorities to issue certain kind of licences, but there are still multiple government agencies involved in appraising and managing FDI projects (Okada 1996, pp. 61–2).

Conclusion

Vietnam's socio-economic reforms that began in 1986, moving it from highly concentrated planning toward a market-oriented economy, has brought much success: high economic growth, inflation control, a decrease in poverty and large amounts of FDI. The factors that explain such large FDI flows in Vietnam since 1988 are the country's advantages of a cheap and well educated labour force, abundant natural resources and a strategic location, as well as the government's positive attitude toward FDI and its protection of domestic infant industries. Moreover, the ownership advantages of MNCs in terms of access to modern technology and know-how, to export markets and financial sources as well as the increasing labour costs in their home countries, have allowed and created the need for MNCs to invest in Vietnam. The decrease of FDI flows to Vietnam since 1997, on the other hand, has been attributed to the regional crisis and the poor physical and economic infrastructure as well as to an inefficient bureaucracy. On balance, FDI flows have significantly promoted socio-economic development in Vietnam. The following chapters elaborate on the impact of FDI on Vietnam's development.

Notes

[1] Vietnam's constitution states that land belongs to the government but Vietnamese individuals have the land use rights. Such rights may be transferred, and used as collateral.

4
The Macroeconomic Impact of FDI in Vietnam

This chapter further examines the impact of FDI on Vietnam's domestic savings and investment, foreign currency earnings, balance of payments and government revenue. Following this, the direct contribution of FDI flows to Gross Domestic Product (GDP) growth will be discussed by looking at the contribution and performance of foreign invested projects (FIPs) as a whole and individually. The decisive role of government policies in making use of FDI flows will be discussed.

FDI and domestic savings and investment

Vietnam's domestic savings level before 1986 was low and the major investment projects during this period were financed mainly by official development assistance (ODA) from socialist countries, especially the former Soviet Union. While reliable data on domestic savings prior to 1986 are not available, in 1988 domestic savings was merely 7.6 percent of GDP (Table 4.1). Such a low level of domestic savings has been attributed to a lack of government policies to promote the development of a private sector, unstable macroeconomic conditions and an inefficient banking and finance system. As a consequence, about 75 percent of private savings had been held in gold, buildings and housing, construction materials and paddy stocks (Harvie and Tran 1997; World Bank 1998, p. 23).

Under such circumstances, FDI flows to Vietnam are considered as important sources of investment capital to supplement national savings and investment. The impact of FDI flows on domestic savings and investment may be through a direct contribution of FDI to gross national investment or indirectly, by creating a better environment for the mobilization domestic savings by generating backward and forward effects and by co-operating with local firms,

Table 4.1 Structure of Capital Formation as Percentage of GDP, 1988–98

	1988	1989	1990	1991	1992	1993	1994	1995	1996	1997	1998
Total	8.1	9.8	15.1	15.1	17.6	25.7	29.3	29.7	29.2	30.9	26.7
Public sector	3.9	6.3	5.1	2.8	5.8	7.0	5.4	11.4	13.2	14.8	14.3
Private sector	3.7	2.3	8.6	9.7	3.9	8.6	15.1	8.7	7.6	6.4	5.7
FDI sector	0.5	1.2	1.5	2.6	7.9	10.1	8.8	9.6	8.3	9.7	6.7
Memo items											
GDP*	15.4	28.1	42.0	76.7	110.5	136.6	170.3	228.9	272.0	313.6	361.0
Exchange rate (000.VND/$)	n.a.	n.a.	5.13	9.27	11.15	10.64	10.98	11.10	11.50	12.94	13.98
Change in GDP deflators	n.a.	n.a.	42.1	72.5	32.6	14.3	14.5	19.5	6.1	6.6	8.9

*: GDP is at current price, VND '000 billion.
Source: Compiled based on data from GSO 1996; 1999a, 1999b, 1999c; IMF 1996, 1999 and various World Bank Country Reports.

either state-owned enterprises (SOEs) or private enterprises (Gupta and Islam 1983; Lee et al. 1986; Borensztein et al. 1995; Fry 1997; Sun 1998). However, FDI may also be detrimental to domestic savings and investment when it competes directly with local entrepreneurs (Frank 1969; Lall and Streeten 1977; Jenkins 1987; Elson 1988; Lim and Fong 1991).

Direct contribution of FDI

The direct contribution of FDI flows to domestic savings and investment can be seen in the total amount of FDI flows and in the contribution of FDI flows to Vietnam's total national capital formation (Table 4.1 and Figure 4.1).

Table 4.1 shows that, while the absolute volume of FDI flows to Vietnam has increased since 1988, FDI flows as a percentage of GDP have also increased and reached their peak of 10.1 percent of GDP in 1993 and then fluctuated around 8–10 percent of GDP between 1994 and 1997, before reducing to 6.7 percent of GDP in 1998. Between 1994–97, FDI flows played a key role in Vietnam's capital formation, accounting for around one-third of gross national investment. After 1995, public investment overtook FDI as the leading investment source because ODA disbursement started to increase significantly and financed several large-scale public investment projects. Figure 4.1 shows that the contribution of FDI as a percentage of GDP in Vietnam was as high as over 60 percent of gross domestic investment in 1992 and 1993. The contribution of FDI to GDP in Vietnam has been higher than that of all the ASEAN countries except Singapore and Malaysia (IMF 1996, p. 52).

Figure 4.1 Gross Domestic Investment and Foreign Direct Investment as Percentage Share of GDP, 1988–98

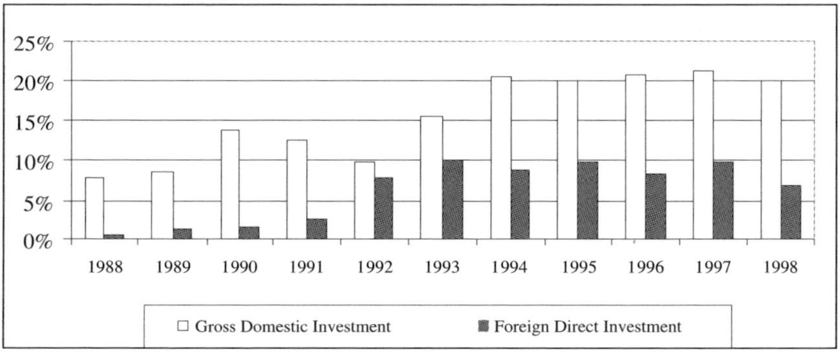

Source: IMF 1996, 1999; GSO 1996; 1999a, 1999b, 1999c.

The direct contribution of FDI to domestic investment comes from three sources:

- The contribution of foreign investors as equity;
- The contribution of Vietnamese partners as equity; and
- FDI projects related to commercial borrowing from overseas.

The contribution of foreign investors and commercial borrowings from overseas in the form of FDI is indicated in Vietnam's balance of payments records (Table 4.2). This infux of foreign currencies has been used to clear project sites, and to import machinery and equipment, materials, modern technologies and know-how and hence contributed to cover the country's foreign exchange gap. Between 1991 and 1997, net FDI flows bridged between 50 to over 80 percent of Vietnam's foreign exchange gap was created by a current account deficit as well as medium and long-term amortization. In these years, FDI flows was the most important foreign currency source for bridging the country's foreign exchange gap, and was many times higher than either ODA or short-term capital.

An important feature of the data on FDI in Vietnam is that they do not fully reflect overseas Vietnamese investors' contributions. Due to differential treatment in terms of taxes, and land use rights between local and foreign investors many overseas Vietnamese have invested in Vietnam under local entrepreneurs' names in order to evade taxes. In Ho Chi Minh City, for example, it is estimated that by 1999, around $16 billion had been invested illegally by overseas Vietnamese investors alone (Bich Ngoc 1999a). If such hidden investment by overseas Vietnamese investors is taken into account, the FDI figures for Vietnam since 1988 would have been higher.

Foreign investment also led to increases in domestic savings by putting more idle capital into effective operation. As shown in Table 4.3, while Vietnam's contribution to joint venture projects in terms of cash, material and machinery accounted for around 15 to 20 percent of the total contribution between 1988–95, the contribution in terms of building, workshop, natural resources value and land and water surface use rights accounted for between 80 to 85 percent of the total (Table 4.3). From 1988 to the end of 1999, except for cancelled projects, the land contribution of Vietnam's partners in legal capital in 660 projects was worth over $1.5 billion. Without FDI, such building, workshop, natural resources, land and water would probably remain unused or underused. Thus, FDI flows have not only mobilized idle assets but have also put them under the effective control and management of multinational corporations (MNCs) (World Bank 1995a, p. 30).

Table 4.2 Vietnam: Balance of Payments, 1986–98[a][b] ($ million)

	1986	1987	1988	1989	1990	1991	1992	1993	1994	1995	1996	1997	1998
1. External balance													
Exports	494	610	733	1,320	1,731	2,042	2,475	2,985	4,054	5,198	7,330	9,145	9,365
Imports	−1,121	−1,184	−1,412	−1,670	−1,775	−2,107	−2,535	−3,532	−5,250	−7,543	−10,483	−10,460	−10,350
Service & transfer (net)	−28	−49	−72	−237	−218	−248	−284	−335	−221	−360	−500	−478	−556
Current account balance	−655	−624	−751	−586	−262	−134	−10	−767	−1,185	−1,928	−2,449	−1,642	−1,073
2. Financing requirements	−943	−908	−1,088	−870	−543	−243	−564	−1,628	−1,853	−2,694	−3,112	−2,495	−2,257
Current account deficit	−655	−624	−751	−586	−262	−134	−10	−767	−1,185	−1,928	−2,449	−1,642	−1,073
Medium & long-term amortization	−265	−233	−363	−350	−279	−104	−175	−652	−547	−733	−729	−804	−1,050
Errors and omissions	−23	−51	26	66	−2	−5	−379	−209	−121	−33	66	−49	−134
3. Financing resources	943	908	1,088	870	543	343	564	1,628	1,853	2,694	3,112	2,495	2,257
ODA disbursements (incl. IMF credit)	513	574	727	763	233	103	540	15	447	535	950	968	1,042
Net FDI flows	n.a.	n.a.	n.a.	100	120	165	333	832	1,048	2,236	1,838	2,003	800
Share of total financing (%)	n.a.	n.a.	n.a.	11.5	22.0	48.1	59.0	51.1	56.6	83.0	59.0	80.3	35.0
Short-term capital (net)	111	37	41	−213	48	19	−41	−313	124	−184	224	−534	−190
Change in net foreign assets (excl. IMF)	2	0	0	−110	−159	−276	−463	477	−292	−439	−441	−265	63
Change in arrears (net)	317	297	320	296	301	332	195	−266	526	546	541	323	129
Debt rescheduling	0	0	0	34	0	0	0	883	0	0	0	0	413

Note: [a] Due to statistical discrepancy, the figures on financing requirements and financing resources in 1991 are not matched.
[b] All the data are at current prices.
Source: World Bank 1995a, 1996, 1999 and GSO 1996, 1999b, 1999c.

Table 4.3 Contribution to Legal Capital, 1988–98

	1988–92	1993	1994	1995	1996	1997	1998
Total ($ million)	**2,095.8**	**1,299**	**1,452**	**2,163**	**1,555**	**1,647**	**631**
Foreign investors ($ million)	**1,174.3**	**884**	**1,078**	**1,591**	**1,137**	**1,248**	**478**
Percentage share (%)	100.0	100.0	100.0	100.0	n.a.	n.a.	n.a.
Money	84.4	58.7	80.7	77.0	n.a.	n.a.	n.a.
Material	1.1	9.2	2.5	4.1	n.a.	n.a.	n.a.
Machinery and equipment	7.4	23.5	13.9	16.9	n.a.	n.a.	n.a.
Others	7.1	8.6	2.9	2.0	n.a.	n.a.	n.a.
Vietnamese partners ($ million)	**921.5**	**415**	**373.7**	**571.3**	**418**	**399**	**153**
Percentage share (%)	100.0	100.0	100.0	100.0	n.a.	n.a.	n.a.
Money	1.1	10.4	11	18.2	n.a.	n.a.	n.a.
Materials	n.a.	n.a.	0.4	0.1	n.a.	n.a.	n.a.
Machinery and equipment	1.0	5.3	6.6	2.6	n.a.	n.a.	n.a.
Houses, workshops	8.6	23.9	15.6	8.7	n.a.	n.a.	n.a.
Natural resource value	81.8	2.2	4.7	2.2	n.a.	n.a.	n.a.
Land & water surface use rights	7.5	58.1	58.7	63.2	n.a.	n.a.	n.a.
Others	—	0.1	3.0	5.0	n.a.	n.a.	n.a.

Source: GSO 1996, 1998.

Moreover, the utilization of such idle assets brought back $152.7 million in 1994 and $167.1 million in 1995 in profits to Vietnam (GSO 1998, pp. 544–51).

In short, the direct contribution of FDI flows to domestic savings and investment in Vietnam has been very important, accounting for between 25 to 45 percent of the country's total. Net FDI flows from overseas also help to cover a large part of the country's foreign currency gap and to finance the current account deficit as well as medium and long-term amortization. Moreover, FDI flows also put otherwise unused assets into operation and hence increase domestic investment.

Indirect impact of FDI

The positive indirect impact of FDI flows on domestic savings and investment can be assessed through the effects of FDI projects that created more favourable conditions for mobilizing domestic savings as well as their backward linkages[2]. As mentioned in Chapter 3, poor infrastructure, including under-developed banking and financial systems, is one of the major reasons that led to a low domestic savings rate. Therefore FDI flows that have been used to develop infrastructure have created a better environment for mobilizing domestic savings.

Recent reviews have indicated that infrastructure development in Vietnam requires an annual investment of around $3 billion or 12 percent of GDP. Annual investment is expected to come from four sources: ODA, the Vietnamese government, FDI and self-financing from state-owned enterprises. Foreign direct investment is estimated to cover one-fifth of such annual investment (World Bank 1998, p. 69). Since 1988, FDI flows have contributed to improving Vietnam's infrastructure by establishing several projects in the areas of power and water supply, and road and port development. Under the Law on Foreign Investment in Vietnam, foreign investors can participate in developing infrastructure either through a business co-operation contract (BCC), joint venture or a build-operation-transfer (BOT) project. From 1988 to the end of 1999, FDI flows were used to finance six BOT projects with total investment capital of $1,321.8 million. FDI also finances the development of several infrastructure projects in Export Processing Zones (EPZs) and Industrial Zones (IZs). By the end of 1999, 14 investment projects for developing EPZ and IZ infrastructure throughout the country had been approved, with total investment capital of $953.5 million. Such important investment has contributed to attracting around $8 billion of committed FDI into EPZ and IZ.

Another indirect impact of FDI flows is to increase ODA commitment and disbursement to Vietnam. Several countries, notably Japan and

France, are Vietnam's largest foreign investors and also the country's biggest aid donors. Several programmes within bilateral ODA commitment have been designed to help foreign investors doing business in Vietnam such as assisting with feasibility studies, and purchasing products produced by FIPs. As FDI flows have increased since the early 1990s, the total ODA commitment has also increased and reached $15.74 billion by 1999 (SRV 1999, pp. 18–19). Table 4.2 also shows the increase of ODA disbursement as it reached a record high $1,042 million in 1998.

Besides infrastructure improvement, FDI flows have also had an indirect positive impact on domestic savings by generating backward effects which promote domestic production. The backward effects of FDI flows in Vietnam may be seen in the agricultural and manufacturing sectors.

In the agricultural sector, the backward effects are the increasing demand for supplies of tropical agricultural products for FDI-related food processing enterprises. Vietnam has comparative advantages in agricultural products such as rice, coffee, tea, sugar, wood, and seafood which attract many foreign investors to Vietnam. By the end of 1999, there were 167 export-intended agricultural processing projects with a total investment capital of $1.93 billion. The development of such foreign invested enterprises (FIEs) has required stable and secure supplies of agricultural materials and hence promoted agricultural production. The government of Vietnam has realised these important indirect effects of FDI flows in the agricultural sector and required foreign investors investing in production and processing dairy products, vegetable oil and sugar as well as wood production to develop raw material sources. By the end of 1999, 26 projects with a total investment of $354.5 million had been approved to operate in those sectors and had generated large backward effects. The country's largest sugar cane processing factory in Nghe An province, for example, will purchase sugar from 10,000 farmers in a cultivated area of 9,000 hectares and an additional 1,000 people are expected to process raw materials and transport the finished products (Bich Ngoc 1999b). Another example is a dairy milk production joint venture project in Song Be province that provided $6.6 million to local breeders to raise dairy cattle and supply milk for the project (Le 1998).

Similarly, in the manufacturing sector, the backward effects are in the development of supporting industries to meet the demand for materials and spare parts by FIEs. The demand for spare parts and accessories has been relatively high in the automobile, motorcycle and electronic industries. The backward effects of FDI flows in the manufacturing sector in Vietnam depend very much on government policies on local content requirements.

For the automobile industry, the local content requirement is 5 percent of the value of the finished vehicle within five years, increasing to 30 percent by the tenth year (UNIDO and DSI 1999, p. 181). Joint ventures that achieve a local content of over 20 percent enjoy a 5 percent tariff rate on imported materials (Masuyama and Mitarai 1998, p. 21). In the motorcycle industry, FIEs are required to achieve a local content of 15–20 percent of value in the first year, increasing to 60–70 percent after 5 years (Luu 2000). The backward effects of FDI flows in the manufacturing industry have been small but increasing. Many local enterprises have been involved in producing spare parts such as tyres, batteries and windscreens for the automobile and motorcycle industries for FIEs. Moreover, several foreign investors have invested in Vietnam to supply spare parts for those industries. By the end of 1998, there were ten projects with total investment capital of $276.8 million operating in Vietnam to meet the demand of FIEs.

However, local content in the motorcycle industry is still below government's expectation. Several foreign parts and accessories manufacturers have found it has been difficult to negotiate with Vietnamese partners to invest in Vietnam, as they are mainly small and medium-sized firms (Masuyama and Mitarai 1998, p. 21). On the other hand, the low effectiveness in implementing government policies is also attributed to the fact that FDI flows may not encourage the development of supportive industries.

In conclusion, FDI flows in Vietnam have produced some positive indirect impacts to promote domestic savings by improving infrastructure and creating backward effects. Several government policies have been introduced to encourage and support such indirect effects. The backward effects generated by FDI flows, however, are still moderate as their focus is mainly on exploiting the country's comparative advantage of cheap labour by concentrating on processing industries that create little added demand for raw materials.

State-owned and private enterprises

The indirect impact of FDI flows on domestic savings, especially the possibility of competition between FIPs and local entrepreneurs, can also be assessed within the relationships between FDI flows, SOEs and private enterprises in the industry and service sectors.

In the agricultural sector, there is no competition between FIPs and local entrepreneurs. At the end of 1998 the direct involvement of FDI in agricultural production was still modest, with 84 projects and total investment of $462.1 million. Such small FDI investment capital (which accounted for 1.5 percent of the total committed investment capital) has had almost no impact on agricultural production as a whole and hence there has been no significant relationship between FDI, SOEs and private enterprises in agricultural production.

The relationship between FDI, SOEs and private enterprises in the industrial and service sectors depends on the existing conditions of SOEs and private enterprises as well as relevant government policies. Such a relationship could be co-operative or competitive depending on circumstances.

First, there is the need for co-operation between SOEs and FIEs for mutual benefit. Before 1986, SOEs played a key role in the industrial and service sectors. However, under central planning, many SOEs were unprofitable and inefficient (UNIDO 1991 in Reinhardt 1993, p. 82; Phan and Nguyen 1996, pp. 6–7). As the country moved toward a market-oriented economy, SOEs have undergone severe reform, in which several loss-making SOEs have been restructured, merged or equitized. As a result, the number of SOEs was reduced from 12,296 in 1989–90 to 5,962 in 1995 (Le and Tran 1996, pp. 6–7). However, the number of unprofitable SOEs remains high, accounting for 60 percent of total SOEs (World Bank 1998, p. 9).

The poor performance of SOEs has been attributed to several reasons such as their reliance on obsolete technology, and their lack of investment capital and access to international markets (UNIDO 1991 cited in Reinhardt 1993, p. 82; Phan and Nguyen 1996, pp. 6–7). The 1993 classification indicated how small Vietnam's SOEs were in terms of investment capital: 49.2 percent of SOEs had capital of less than $0.1 million; 26.6 percent had between $0.1 million and $0.3 million; 16.3 percent had between $0.3 and $1 million; 7.9 percent had between $0.3 and $1 million; and 7.9 percent had capital in excess of $1 million (Nguyen et al. 1996, p. 26). The machinery and equipment in SOEs have been considered as obsolete as two to five generations compared to international standards (Bezanson et al. 1999, p. 63). Meagre capital and obsolete technology hindered SOEs' development and their penetration of international markets. Given the circumstances, FDI flows have been considered as a vital source of capital, technology and access to international market for SOEs.

Despite their shortcomings, SOEs possess characteristics that are crucial to the successful operation of FDI in Vietnam:

- SOEs have better access to land;
- compared to Vietnam's private sector, SOEs are bigger in terms of capital, and have better facilities;
- SOEs have a closer relationship with government and policymakers; and
- SOEs have better knowledge of the local market (UNIDO and DSI 1997, p. 29).

The importance of these factors has also been confirmed by a survey of 19 Australian firms investing in Vietnam (Maitland 1996, p. 102). By the end of 1998, joint ventures between foreign investors and SOEs accounted for over 74 percent of total committed FDI. In short, the plight of SOEs has made co-operation, rather than competition, between SOEs and FDI vital for both SOEs and foreign investors to achieve mutual benefit.

Second, while there is a need for co-operation between SOEs and FIEs, there is also little possibility of competition between the local private sector and FIPs. The state of Vietnam's private sector has made it unlikely that the majority of private enterprises could be direct competitors. In Vietnam, private enterprises have been always smaller than SOEs—the number of private enterprises employing fewer than 100 workers accounted for 91.7 percent of the total in 1997 (GSO 1999, cited in MPDF 1999a, p. 69). The private sector has developed fapidly since 1986 with the rate of annual increase in the number of private enterprises remaining as high as 66 percent in 1994 and between 24–40 percent between 1995–97 (GSO 1999). Such high growth rates can be largely attributed to the change in government policies in moving towards a market-oriented economy and recognizing the importance of the private sector (World Bank 1995a, pp. 24–5).

The small size and labour-intensive nature of private enterprise in Vietnam has encouraged their participation in sectors where size and scale are not significant cost advantages. They target mainly the medium and low end of the domestic market while leaving the high-end domestic market for either imported products or products produced by FIEs. There is also less competition between FIEs and large local private enterprises for the domestic market. Large private enterprises which employ more than 100 full-time workers operate in labour-intensive sectors like garments, footwear, plastic products and seafood, account for around 8 percent of the total private sector in manufacturing, and are highly export orientated (World Bank 1999b, p. 12). On average, those enterprises export about 75 percent of their production (MPDF 1999, cited in World Bank 1999b, p. 12).

Many surveys on the development of the private sector in Vietnam have identified several obstacles that have constrained its development, none of them identified with FDI flows. A survey of 95 large private enterprises, which were most likely to face competition from FIEs, revealed that several problems other than competition by FIEs have constrained their development (Table 4.4).

Another survey, conducted in 1997 by the Japan International Co-operation Agency and Ministry of Planning and Investment in seven

Table 4.4 Problems for the Development of Private Enterprises

Problems	Percentage of respondents
Difficult access to investment capital	53 percent of respondents
Lack of information	41 percent of respondents
Insufficient working capital	39 percent of respondents
Asian regional economic crisis	19 percent of respondents
Unclear government policies	16 percent of respondents

Source: MPDF 1999a, p. 30.

regions, found that the most important issues for the development of the private sector were:

- access to financial credit;
- a more streamlined tax system;
- strengthening of government investment funds;
- simplifying administrative procedures;
- technological support;
- export finance; and
- access to foreign market information (Ebashi, Sakai and Takada 1998, p. 50).

These surveys showed that FDI flows may actually supplement sources of investment capital, modern technology and know-how and access to international markets that are needed for the development of the private sector.

While the existing conditions of SOEs and private enterprises allow and require co-operation with FDI, government policies also promote such co-operation and minimize the competition. In general, government policies have changed toward creating a level playing field for both SOEs and the private sector in terms of tax policies, access to the international market and, especially, access to capital. The government also promotes co-operation between the private sector and FDI as seen by the rise in the committed capital of joint ventures with the private sector, from 0.9 percent of total committed FDI in 1991 to 5 percent in 1998 (Table 3.3).

In terms of incentives, the government has made several attempts to provide a level playing field for both FIEs and local enterprises. While FIEs have been given several incentives regarding profit tax, personal income tax and export–import tax, domestic enterprises enjoy several advantages in terms of capital, land hire, government subsidies (mainly for SOEs) and export requirements. Regarding profit tax, FIEs enjoy ordinary profit tax of 25 percent compared to 32 percent for local enterprises, and profit tax can be reduced to as low as 10–20 percent for priority projects compared to 15–25 percent for local enterprises of the same category. Also, the tax holiday could be as long as eight years for FIEs compared to local enterprises.

Domestic enterprises, on the other hand, can establish either a limited or an unlimited liability company, with no limit on operation duration—as compared to FIEs that can be established as limited liability companies only with operations of no longer than 50 years or, in some special cases, 70 years. Local enterprises can also contribute to investment capital by either land use rights or local currency, can issue shares to mobilize investment capital, enjoy lower fees for water and electricity supply, telecommunications and land hire, and receive government subsidies in terms of low interest rates. Moreover, in order to promote co-operation between FDI and local enterprises, the government also limits foreign investors to establishing only joint ventures or BCCs, not 100 percent foreign-owned firms, in the strategic sectors mentioned in Box 1. The government has also gone further to reduce competition by requiring FIEs to export at least 80 percent of their production output for the products that domestic enterprises have already produced at the same quality and with which they have met local demand. The list of such products may change over time (see Box 2 for the 1999 list).

Box 1
Sectors Excluded from Establishing 100 Percent Foreign-Owned Enterprises

1. Establishment and operation of international and domestic telecommunication system (only allowed for BCCs)
2. Exploitation and processing of oil and gas and precious mineral resources
3. Building and operation of infrastructure in industrial zones, export processing zones and high-tech zones
4. Construction
5. Air-borne, railway and sea-borne transportation, passenger transportation, building of ports and airports (there are different regulations for build-operation-transfer, build-transfer-operation and build-transfer projects)
6. Cement and steel production
7. Industrial explosives production
8. Plantation, including long-term industrial crops
9. Back-packer tourism
10. Cultural, sports, and leisure activities

Source: NPPH 1999, p. 288.

> **Box 2**
> **List of Industrial Products, at Least 80 percent of Which Must be Exported**
>
> 1. Motorbikes
> 2. Cars, or small trucks of less than 10 tons
> 3. Irrigation pumps with capacities of less than 30,000 cubic metres per hour, ordinary pumps of less than 540 cubic metres per hour
> 4. Medium and low voltage electrical cables
> 5. Ordinary telecommunication cables
> 6. Vessels with a capacity of less than 30,000 tons, fishing ships of less than 1000 c.v. and other inland water transport means
> 7. Audio-video products
> 8. Aluminum bars
> 9. Construction steel bars with diametres of less than 40 mm
> 10. Bath tiles and toilet ceramics
> 11. NPK fertilizer
> 12. Detergent
> 13. Ordinary and construction paint
> 14. Batteries (lead and acid)
> 15. PVC
> 16. Bicycle and motorbike tubes and tires
> 17. Soda (NaOH) and Acid (H_2SO_4, HCL)
> 18. Electrical fans
> 19. Bicycles and accessories
> 20. Transformers of less than 35 KV
> 21. Diesel engines of less than 15 c.v.
> 22. Garments
> 23. Footwear
> 24. Ordinary plastic products
>
> *Source*: NPPH 1999, p. 335.

Government policies in general and the policies related to the operation of FIEs seem to work very effectively in limiting the crowding-out effects of FDI flows. Statistical data as well as results of the 1995 economic survey and 1998 industrial survey revealed that despite FDI flows to Vietnam having increased rapidly since 1990, SOEs and private enterprises in the industrial sector—which received over 63 percent of FDI flows in Vietnam—still achieved high growth rates in terms of number of employees and revenue (Tables 4.5 and 4.6)

Table 4.5 Major Indicators of Industrial Enterprises, 1995 and 1998 (percent)

	30 Jun 1995			30 Jun 1998		
	SOEs	Private enterprises	FIEs	SOEs	Private enterprises	FIEs
Number of enterprises	2,382	6,215	395	1,281	559,706	830
Number of employees ('000)	724	246.7	74.5	745.08	1,682.5	242.1
Total capital ($ million as at 31/12/1994 and 31/12/1997)	4,614.6	517.3	3,606.6	9,901.0	1,639.3	9,312.6

Note: Exchange rates of Vietnam Dong (VND) 10,978 and 12,938 per $1 have been used to convert data from VND to $ in 1994 and 1997.
Source: GSO 1999b, 1999c.

Table 4.6 Industrial Output Growth Rate, 1989–98 (percent)

Private	1989	1990	1991	1992	1993	127.0	127.0	1996	1997	1998	1999	2000	2001
SOEs	−2.5	6.1	11.9	20.6	14.6	124.7	13.9	11.9	10.8	7.9	5.4	13.2	12.7
Private sector	−4.3	−0.7	7.4	9.6	8.1	11.2	14.0	11.5	9.5	6.7	10.9	19.2	20.3
FDI sector				23.3	302	153.2	127.1	21.7	23.2	23.3		21	21.8	12.1

Source: Complied from various GSO Statistical Yearbooks and World Bank 2002.

Between 1995 and 1998, the number of industrial SOEs fell by 1,101 enterprises as the result of the process of restructuring SOEs. However, the number of employees increased by 21,052 workers or about 3 percent of the total employees in 1998 and total capital almost doubled. In the private sector, there was a more than ninetyfold increase in the number of enterprises, a sevenfold increase in the number of workers and a more than threefold increase in investment capital. Figure 4.2 shows that capital outlay increased in all major industrial sectors for all SOEs, private sector and FIEs between 1994 and 1998. This means that there was not much competition between them, but that they did respond positively to market opportunity and government reforms.

Such increases have also been seen in industrial output growth, where both SOEs and private enterprises achieved very high growth rates between 1991 and 2001 as shown in Table 4.6.

52 *Foreign Direct Investment and Development in Vietnam*

Despite the high growth rate of SOEs and private enterprises, the large FDI flows and high growth rate of FIEs may possess some potential threats to the development of SOEs and private enterprises in some industries. It was estimated that by 2000, FIEs would produce two-thirds of the total detergent output and 80 percent of the beverage market (Nguyen 1996b, pp. 19–24).

Figure 4.2 The Growth Rate of Industrial Capital Outlay of Major Industries, 1994–98

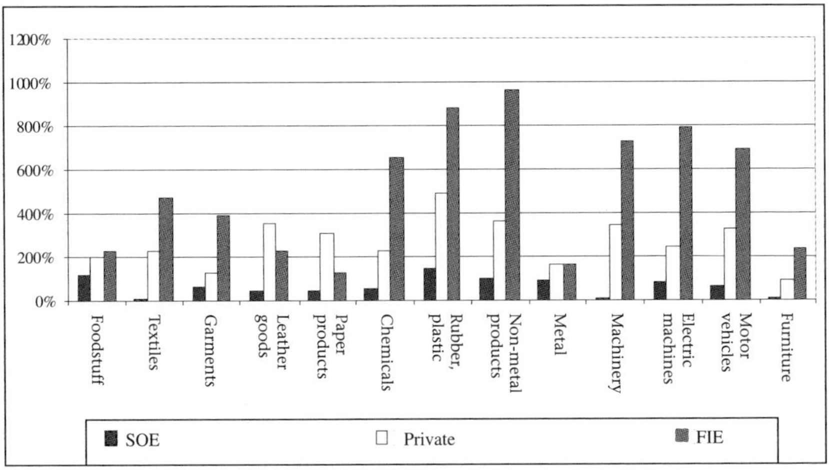

Source: IMF 1998, 1999c.

A typical example of competition between FDI and local enterprises may be seen in the hotel industry during the Asian regional economic crisis. As a result of Vietnam's open door policy and high economic growth rate, the number of foreigners visiting Vietnam increased from 440,000 in 1992 to 1.7 million in 1997 (GSO 1999b). Such increases in the number of visitors have attracted large amounts of investment in the hotel industry from both local and foreign investors. Between 1988 and 1998, 107 foreign-invested projects with total investment capital of $3.4 billion were approved. Such FDI flows in the hotel industry increased the number of foreign-invested hotels from 15 in 1993 to 49 in 1997 with a total capacity of 5,716 rooms, mainly classified as three-star or above (GSO 1996, GSO 1999b). For the hotel industry as a whole, the number of rooms increased rapidly from 50,000 in 1995 to 62,000 in 1999 (VTA 2000). However, as the number of foreign investors did not increase significantly between 1996 and 1998 due to the regional economic crisis, several hotels were left empty. The occupancy rate fell from 51 percent in 1995 to 43 percent in 1999 (Ngo 1999). In 1998, for example, the occupancy rate of hotels in Hanoi decreased by 15–25 percent for foreign-invested hotels, 10–20 percent for state-owned hotels and 5 percent for private hotels (Nguyen 1999b). As a consequence, several foreign-invested hotels have competed directly with locally owned mini-hotels by reducing hotel room rates or providing other incentives. Luxury hotel room rates have fallen by an average of 30–50 percent and even as much as 70 percent in some cases (Nguyen 1999b).

Serious competition in the hotel industry has been attributed to the regional crisis and hence the reduction of foreign visitors to Vietnam. However, a more efficient government management and strategy to develop the hotel industry may ease this competition and improve the operational efficiency within the industry.

The competition between FIEs and local enterprises may also be seen in the increasing trend of switching from joint venture to 100 percent foreign-owned enterprises since 1997. Since the introduction of the Law on Foreign Investment in Vietnam up to the end of 1999 (except for cancelled projects), 53 projects have changed their investment form, of which 43 cases (accounting for 81.1 percent of the total) occurred between 1997 and 1999. Of those 43 cases, 42 projects with a total investment capital of $677.4 million changed into 100 percent foreign-owned, while only one project with total investment capital of $0.7 million changed into a joint venture. The reasons behind this trend are changes in government policy, better knowledge of Vietnam's market of foreign investors, a conflict of interest and the limited capacity of Vietnamese partners.

Since the regional crisis, the government of Vietnam has made several attempts to further liberalize the investment laws in order reverse the decline in FDI flows, relaxing restrictions on establishing 100 percent foreign-owned enterprises. Also, after operating as a joint venture for a while, foreign investors have secured the land, gained better knowledge about the law, regulations, and local market and established important connections in Vietnam. Hence they no longer need Vietnamese partners. Another reason is the limited capacity of Vietnamese partners in joint ventures as their contribution has accounted for around only 30 percent—which has been mainly in terms of land use rights. Moreover, there are some conflicts of interest between foreign investors and Vietnamese partners and "due to lack of capable representatives in joint ventures, the Vietnamese side is often cheated on, leading to losses" (VIR 1998a). As Vietnam's representatives in these joint ventures have not had the capability to manage the joint venture operation thoroughly as well as having to operate under unclear regulations, many foreign investors in several joint ventures have managed to swallow up local partners through "strategic losses". Local partners in those joint ventures have blamed foreign partners for intentionally causing losses and imposing such losses on local partners in order to force them out of the joint ventures (Lao Dong 2000).

In conclusion, state-owned enterprises and private enterprises have had to co-operate for mutual benefit. Government policies, on the other hand, have also promoted such co-operation and minimized competition in order to promote domestic savings and investment. FDI flows, therefore, have directly and indirectly helped to mobilize domestic savings and investment. Where FIEs compete with local enterprises, such negative effects are small compared to the positive effects. However, the increasing trend of changing the investment form from a joint venture toward 100 percent foreign-owned may require close government monitoring in order to minimize possible negative effects on domestic savings and investment.

Impact on the balance of payments

Like other developing countries, Vietnam has faced foreign currency shortages during its development created by low levels of exports, heavy dependence on imports of raw material and consumer goods, and a huge debt burden. This section examines the impact of FDI flows on Vietnam's exports and imports and other foreign currency flows, and on the country's foreign debt burden.

Impact on exports and imports

Before 1986, Vietnam's foreign trade was mainly with Eastern European countries and especially the former Soviet Union: Vietnam maintained large trade deficits that were covered by ODA from those countries. Since the reforms, Vietnam's exports and imports have increased rapidly at an annual growth rate of 20 percent, while the trade deficit has been kept under control (Table 3.1) thanks to the government's moves towards a market oriented economy. However, Vietnam's exports have been dominated by unprocessed or semi-processed agricultural products, or labour-intensive manufacturing products with low added value (Than and Tan 1993; Fforde and deVylder 1996; Harvie and Tran 1997).

Foreign direct investment has contributed to the increases in Vietnam's exports by providing necessary investment capital, know-how and modern technology, as well as access to international markets through FIPs. Table 4.7 shows that exports generated by FIPs increased as much as 127.7 percent in 1997, many times higher than the growth rate of the country's exports in general. Even in 1998, when Vietnam's exports grew at the low rate of only 2.4 percent due to the Asian regional economic crisis, the exports of FIPs remained at 10.7 percent.

The share of FIPs' exports in the country's total exports also increased steadily from 2.5 percent in 1991 to 24.2 percent in 1999.

Foreign invested projects' access to international markets, modern technology and management skills have made them one of the key factors in Vietnam's export growth. The contribution of FIPs to Vietnam's exports increased from 2.9 percent in 1992 to 13.7 percent in 1997 before reducing to 2.1 percent in 1998 and 6.5 percent in 1999. Over the 1991–98 period, FIPs contributed to about 9.5 percent of Vietnam's export growth (Table 4.7). The list of export products of FIPs also reflects the country's comparative advantage in producing agricultural products and labour-intensive products. Other than crude oil, the major export products of FIPs in are electronic products, footwear, garments, seasonings and organic products, household electronic products, seafood, coffee and rice.

Conversely, the import volume of FIPs has also increased rapidly, with a growth rate of 144.5 percent in 1995 (Table 4.7). However, the imports of FIPs decreased in 1998 and 1999 as a consequence of the regional crisis and lower demand for Vietnam's export products. The rapid increase in FIPs' imports before 1998 led to large trade deficits. In 1996, for example, the FIPs' trade deficit was $1.2 billion, accounting for 40 percent of the country's trade deficit. However, this figure increased to 83.7 percent of the country's trade deficit as the government tightened imports and reduced non-FIPs' trade deficit by $1.7 billion, while FIPs' trade deficit reduced by only $156 million. The FIPs trade deficit then turned into a surplus of $582 million in 1999. In general, the volume of imports of FIPs have accounted for a large share of the country's trade deficit. However, the trade deficit created by FIPs is not as serious as in the case of China, where FIPs' imports were many times higher than exports (as much as seven times in 1985) (Chen 1999, pp. 80–82). Moreover, closer examination has revealed that equipment and machinery necessary for their operations in Vietnam have accounted for a large part of FIPs' imports. Between 1988 and June 1996, the contribution of foreign investors to the legal capital of joint ventures in the form of equipment and machinery was 19 percent, ranked second after the contribution by cash (GSO 1996, p. 104). If such imports of machinery and equipment were to be excluded, the trade deficit of FIPs would become less serious. The reduction of FIPs' imports of machinery and equipment between 1995–96 and 1998–99 that reflected the declining trend of FDI flows to Vietnam actually turned FIPs trade balance from a deficit into a surplus.

Moreover, the imports of raw materials necessary for FIPs to create products for the domestic market may create a trade deficit but, on the other hand, it surely has saved foreign currency that had been used in the past to import either finished products for the local market or raw

Table 4.7 Share of FIPs' Exports and Imports in Total Exports and Imports of Vietnam, 1991–99

	1991	1992	1993	1994	1995	1996	1997	1998	1999
FIPs' exports ($m)	52	112	257	352	440	786	1,790	1,982	2,591
Growth rate of FIPs' exports (%)	n.a.	115.4	129.5	37.0	25.0	78.6	127.7	10.7	30.7
Share in country's exports (%)	2.5	4.5	8.6	8.7	8.5	10.7	19.6	21.2	24.2
Contribution to country's export growth*	n.a.	2.9	5.9	3.2	2.2	6.7	13.7	2.1	6.5
FIPs' imports ($m)	n.a.	n.a.	n.a.	600.5	1,468	2,042.7	2,890	2,668	2,009
Growth rate of FIPs' imports (%)	n.a.	n.a.	n.a.	n.a.	144.5	39.1	41.5	-7.7	-24.7
Share in country's imports (%)	n.a.	n.a.	n.a.	11.4	19.5	19.5	27.6	25.8	19.9
FIPs' trade deficit ($m)	n.a.	n.a.	n.a.	-248.5	-1,028	-1,256.7	-1,100	-686	582
Share in country's trade deficit (%)	n.a.	n.a.	n.a.	-20.8	-43.8	-39.9	-83.7	-69.6	97.0

*FIPs' contribution in year t = $\frac{\text{(FIPs exports in year t − FIPs exports in year t-1)}}{\text{Country's exports in year t-1}}$

Source: World Bank 1995a, 1996, 1999; GSO 1996, 1999b; MOT 1999.

materials for local producers. During the 1995–97 period, when the economy of Vietnam was growing at a very high rate, the imports of some products of which FIPs dominate the production actually decreased. For example, the imports of motor vehicles reduced by 31 percent, lubricating oil by 54 percent, sodium glutamate by 5 percent, televisions by 86.7 percent and motorcycles by 67.5 percent (GSO 1999b, pp. 282–3). Nevertheless, the large import volume of materials for FIPs has shown that Vietnam does not have sufficient supportive industries to provide materials and other supplies which are up to international standard.

Besides generating foreign currency income through the export of goods, FIPs also help to increase the country's foreign currency income through tourism activities and other services. In 1993, for example, the foreign currency income of FIPs in the tourism industry was $20.8 million, accounting for 23.5 percent of the total foreign currency income of the whole industry, while in 1997, the turnover of FIPs in the tourism and hotel industry was $760 million (GSO 1998, p. 789; GSO 1999a, p. 269).

Other effects of FDI on the balance of payments

Other effects of FDI flows on the balance of payments include the generation of debt for Vietnam and the outflows of foreign currencies as remittances.

Of the total FDI implementation between 1991–98, foreign loans were $4,538 million, accounting for 31 percent of total FDI implementation as detailed in Table 4.8.

Of those loans, about 50 percent are long-term loans and 90 percent of the loans have actually come from parent companies and 10 percent from international financial organizations (GSO 1999c, p. 245). Compared to the loans taken on by local firms, such loans committed by FIPs have more favourable conditions. In general, the payment terms of FIPs loans are over seven years and interest rates are about one percent higher than the London inter-bank offer rate[2] (World Bank 1997b, p. 32). Those loans, however, have not seriously deepened the debt situation of Vietnam. The total external debt burden of Vietnam as at December 1998 stood at $18.8 billion and the annual debt service of Vietnam is estimated at around 16 percent of the country's exports, or between 5–7 percent of GDP, well within the manageable range (World Bank 1998, p. 79; IMF 1999; OECF 1999).

To service their loans, every year FIPs have paid the interest and principal that were $338 million and $314 million respectively in 1998. However, the IMF had estimated that in 2001, Vietnam paid $151 million for interest and $894 million for principal (IMF 1999, p. 12). Such a

Table 4.8 Foreign Loans Classified by Form of Investment, 1991–98 ($ million)

	1991	1992	1993	1994	1995	1996	1997	1998	1991–98
Total	10	38	238	594	989	921	1,072	560	4,538
100 % Foreign-owned	0	4	47	95	208	263	333	35	977
Joint venture	8	20	95	273	431	626	706	170	2,369
Business co-operation contract	2	14	97	226	350	32	32	355	1,194
Build-operation-transfer	0	0	0	0	0	0	0	0	–2

Source: State Bank of Vietnam data in IMF 1999, Table II. 6, p. 10.

large debt service may influence the balance of payments situation of Vietnam.

Another source of foreign currency outflows as a consequence of FDI flows is the remittance in terms of salaries and wages of foreigners working in Vietnam, as well as the dividend on foreign contributions. It is estimated that between 6,000–7,000 foreigners have been working in FIPs with monthly wages and salaries of between $1,000 to $2,000, many times higher than those of local workers.

The payment of dividends on foreign contribution, however, depends on the performance of FIPs as foreign investors can receive dividends only when the FIPs make profits. Such dividend payments were $429 million in 1998 and are expected to be around $400 million for the period from 2000 to 2004 (IMF 1999, p. 12). The government of Vietnam has encouraged foreign investors to reinvest their profit in Vietnam by providing tax incentives on profit reinvested in Vietnam and imposing taxes on remittances. The remittance tax rates are 5 percent, 7 percent and 10 percent depending on the size of the capital contribution of foreign investors. However, if the profit is reinvested in Vietnam, foreign investors will receive a refund of profit tax on the amount of reinvested profit and the specific rates of refund (50 percent, 75 percent and 100 percent) will depend on the priority level of foreign investment projects (NPPH 1999, p. 51). By the end of 1999, about 30 FIPs had reinvested their profit to expand their production (VNN 1999).

Moreover, under the pressure of the Asian regional economic crisis, the government required all profit-making FIPs to sell 80 percent of their hard currency reserves to the State Bank of Vietnam. The ratio has since been reduced to 50 percent (Ha Thang 1999). This short-term solution was designed to minimize the pressure on the country's foreign currency reserves, especially during the regional financial crisis, and hence maintain macroeconomic stability.

In conclusion, FDI flows have had the effect of increasing exports by providing access to the international market, especially for manufactured exports, modern technology and know-how, and investment capital. However, such increases have been largely offset by huge amounts of imports of FIPs. Nevertheless, when the imports of machinery and equipment are disregarded, the deficit in the trade account of FIPs appears to have been less serious, or even in surplus in 1999. On the capital account, while foreign investors have brought into Vietnam a large amount of investment capital, they have also created a large amount of debt and debt service obligations as well as outflows of foreign currency in remittances. However, the favourable terms of FIPs loans have made such debt manageable. Moreover, the government of Vietnam has tried to reduce foreign currency outflows by encouraging foreign investors to reinvest their profit in Vietnam through several tax incentives.

Contribution to government revenue

Another macroeconomic impact of FDI flows is their contribution to the government budget and therefore to the reduction of the fiscal gap. Before 1986, the government of Vietnam always faced a fiscal deficit. While government expenditure programmes were very ambitious, covering large capital intensive projects and subsidies for SOEs, government income was very limited and had been financed by ODA from Eastern European countries. The government had to use high inflation as a means to cover its large fiscal gap and finance its ambitious expenditure (Than and Tan 1993; Fforde and deVylder 1996; Harvie and Tran 1997). Since 1986, the fiscal balance has improved thanks to the abolition of the subsidy system, tax reforms and the contribution of FIPs to government revenue through turnover tax, profit tax, income tax, import–export tax and remittance tax. Figure 4.3 shows the increasing contribution of FIPs to government revenue from 0.02 percent of GDP in 1991 to 1.2 percent of GDP in 1997 and 1998.

In the industrial sector (including manufacturing, mineral and water, gas and electricity generation and supply), the contribution of FIPs to government revenue also increased from $456.08 million in 1994 to $809.9 million in 1997. The share of FIPs' contribution within the total industrial contribution to government revenue increased from 34.6 percent in 1994 to 49.2 percent in 1997 (GSO 1999b, c).

The low percentage share of FIPs' contribution to the government budget is attributed to the fact that many of them have just started their operations and are still in the tax deduction period. Moreover, in order to promote exports, the government has allowed zero tax on the imports of machinery and equipment and materials for producing export products

Figure 4.3 Vietnam's Budgetary Contribution, 1990–98

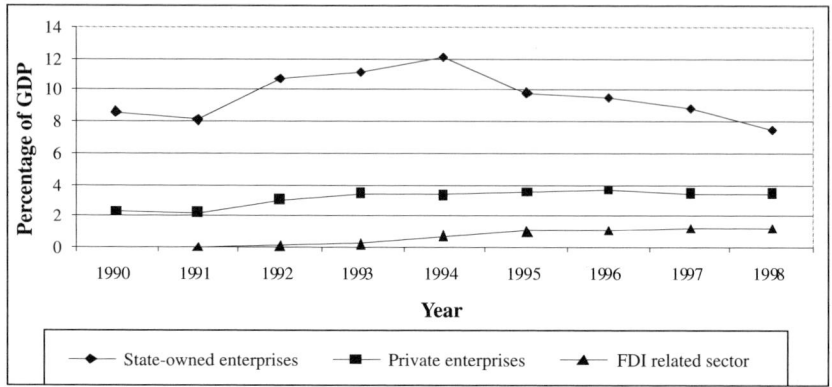

Source: Ministry of Finance and several Statistical Yearbooks in World Bank 1999b; GSO 1999.

which also lowers the government income from FIPs. By the end of 1998, the government of Vietnam had given tax preference to 523 FIPs (STD 1999). Hence, while the volume of FIPs' contribution to government revenue almost doubled between 1994 and 1997, the contribution per sale actually declined. While the contribution of FIPs to the government budget has been small, it has become an important source of government revenue.

FDI and economic growth

The previous sections examined the impact of FDI flows on domestic savings and investment, on generating foreign currency earnings and on government revenue. Overall, FDI flows have contributed to covering, to varying extents, the savings–investment, foreign exchange and fiscal gaps, and hence they have promoted economic growth. This section will examine how FDI flows contribute to the economic growth of Vietnam by looking at the role of FDI flows in several government development projections, by estimating their direct contribution to economic growth and, finally, by reviewing the performance of FIPs.

In the government projections for socio-economic development up to the year 2000, FDI was considered as one of the major sources of investment capital. In order to achieve the target of doubling the 1990s GDP per capita by the year 2000 and hence an average annual GDP growth rate of 8 percent for the whole period, total investment of $40 billion was needed. Of that $40 billion investment fund, 51 percent would have come from domestic sources and 49 percent from external sources—and a projected FDI flow of $12–13 billion would have been needed (SRV 1993, pp. 73–4). In the accelerated growth plan for 1996–2000, the annual target growth of 9–10 percent was set and estimated FDI flows of $13 billion would have been needed to make up the total investment of $41–42 billion (SRV 1996, pp. 13–14).

Several of the World Bank's short-term projections for Vietnam's socio-economic development have considered FDI flows as a major source of investment. In its 1999 projection, the World Bank has estimated that, in order to achieve the annual GDP growth rate of 4–5 percent for 2000, 5.5–6 percent for 2001 and 6–7 percent for 2002, estimated FDI flows of $0.75 billion, $0.85 billion and $1.03 billion would have been needed for 2000, 2001 and 2002 (World Bank 1999b, p.50). In general, FDI is projected to account for around one-third of the country's financing requirements (World Bank 1999b, p. 50)

However, estimating the direct contribution of FDI flows on GDP growth is no simple task. As FDI flows began in Vietnam in 1988, the data on FDI flows do not cover a long enough period to establish the time series regression analysis to test the correlation between FDI flows and GDP growth. Another way to estimate the direct contribution of FDI flows to GDP growth is to use the Harrod-Domar model and to examine the structural share of FIPs in Vietnam's GDP.

The Harrod-Domar model allows us to estimate the contribution of FDI flows to GDP growth based on the data of the share of FDI flows in GDP and the Incremental Capital Output Ratio (ICOR). The determination of ICOR in Vietnam is a complicated issue. In several projections, an ICOR of 3 has been used by the government of Vietnam and international organizations to calculate the necessary investment fund. However, such an ICOR is low compared to China, the country that shares several conditions with Vietnam, where an ICOR of 4 has been used to project long-term economic development (Harvie and Tran 1997, p. 67). For FDI projects that tend to use more modern, and hence expensive equipment, an ICOR of 5 may be appropriate in for Vietnam. Based on the data on the FDI flows as a share of GDP provided in Table 4.1, the direct contribution of FDI flows to GDP growth has been calculated by using the Harrod-Domar model with an ICOR of 5 (Table 4.9). In this case, the direct contribution of FDI flows to GDP growth increased from 0.1 percent in 1988 to around 2 percent during the 1993–97 period before reducing to 1.3 percent in 1998.

The application of the Harrod-Domar model faces the problem of time lags, where FDI flows may not generate any impact on GDP growth until the construction work to establish FIPs has been finished. In the case of FDI flows in Vietnam, the construction duration is about five years for the oil and gas industry; four years for hotels and offices, the cement industry, and for establishing infrastructure for industrial zones, two years for transport, telecommunication and manufacturing, and one year for light industry (Do 1996, p. 6).

Table 4.9 Contribution of Foreign Direct Investment to GDP Growth

	1988	1989	1990	1991	1992	1993	1994	1995	1996	1997	1998
GDP real growth rate (percentage)	5.9	8.0	5.1	6	8.6	8.1	8.8	9.5	9.3	8.2	5.8
Based on the Harrod-Domar model											
FDI flows as share of GDP	0.5	1.2	1.5	2.6	7.9	10.1	8.8	9.6	8.3	9.7	6.7
ICOR	5	5	5	5	5	5	5	5	5	5	5
FDI contribution to GDP growth (percentage point)	0.1	0.24	0.3	0.5	1.6	2.0	1.8	1.9	1.7	1.9	1.3
Based on the structure of GDP											
GDP at 1994 price (VND billion)	n.a.	n.a.	n.a	n.a.	144,761	156,487	170,258	195,567	213,833	231,264	244,676
State sector (VND billion)	n.a.	n.a.	n.a	n.a.	n.a.	n.a	71,620	78,367	87,207	95,638	100,879
Collective sector (VND billion)	n.a.	n.a.	n.a	n.a.	n.a.	n.a	18,164	18,978	19,654	20,173	20,782

(continued)

Table 4.9 Contribution of Foreign Direct Investment to GDP Growth (continued)

	1988	1989	1990	1991	1992	1993	1994	1995	1996	1997	1998
Private sector (VND billion)	n.a.	n.a.	n.a	n.a.	n.a.	n.a	5,469	5,978	6,838	7,507	8,088
Household (VND billion)	n.a.	n.a.	n.a	n.a.	n.a.	n.a	64,025	70,287	74,913	79,128	82,594
Mixed (VND billion)	n.a.	n.a.	n.a	n.a.	n.a.	n.a	7,812	8,802	9,511	9,848	10,162
FDI sector (VND billion)	n.a.	n.a.	n.a	n.a.	2,895	5,634	11,441	13,155	15,709	18,970	2,2171
Contribution to GDP growth (percentage)											
State sector	n.a.	n.a.	n.a	n.a.	n.a.	n.a	n.a.	4.0	4.5	3.9	2.3
Collective sector	n.a.	n.a.	n.a	n.a.	n.a.	n.a	n.a.	0.5	0.3	0.2	0.3
Private sector	n.a.	n.a.	n.a	n.a.	n.a.	n.a	n.a.	0.3	0.4	0.3	0.3
Household	n.a.	n.a.	n.a	n.a.	n.a.	n.a	n.a.	3.7	2.4	2.0	1.5
Mixed	n.a.	n.a.	n.a	n.a.	n.a.	n.a	n.a.	0.6	0.4	0.2	0.1
FDI sector	n.a.	n.a.	n.a	n.a.	n.a.	1.9	3.7	1.0	1.3	1.5	1.4

Note: FDI sector contribution in year t = (FDI sector share of GDP in year t − FDI sector share of GDP in year t-1) / GDP of year t-1
Due to changes in the constant price system used to calculate GDP, there was a large increase in 1995's GDP compared to 1994's GDP.
Source: Compiled based on data from GSO 1996; 1999a, 1999b, 1999c; IMF 1996, 1999.

Table 4.10 Major Industrial Products, 1995–98

Products	1995				1996				1997				1998			
		Share in Total (%)				Share in Total (%)				Share in Total (%)				Share in Total (%)		
	Total	SOEs	Private	FIPs	Total	SOEs	Private	FIPs	Total	SOEs	Private	FIPs	Total	SOEs	Private	FIPs
Crude oil (000. tons)	7,620	0.0	0.0	100.0	8,803	0.0	0.0	100	10,090	0.0	0.0	100.0	12,500	0.0	0.0	100.0
Canned fruits (tons)	12,784	43.9	0.0	56.1	16,318	76.3	0.5	23.2	21,422	69.6	0.0	33.7	23,550	63.9	0.0	36.1
Vegetable oil (tons)	38,612	64.6	35.4	0.1	78,076	39.5	21.0	39.5	87,718	48.1	17.2	34.7	98,163	51.3	16.5	32.3
Beer (mill. litres)	465	67.5	3.2	29.2	533	68.5	5.3	26.3	581	67.5	5.9	26.7	656.1	67.9	5.5	26.6
Fabrics (mill. metres)	263	57.0	27.4	15.6	285	53.3	22.1	24.6	298.6	51.2	26.9	21.9	316.6	52.4	26.0	21.6
Garments (000. pieces)	171,900	42.1	42.3	15.6	206,959	34.2	55.3	10.5	302,192	27.5	36.4	36.1	289,923	28.6	30.7	40.7
Soft leather (000. sheets)	1,383	0.0	70.9	29.1	1,226	52.1	7.1	40.8	2,970	77.3	0.4	22.3	3065	76.7	0.5	22.8
Detergent (000. tons)	129	72.1	10.1	17.8	167	58.7	12.0	29.3	213.3	56.0	15.0	29.0	216	55.6	15.3	29.2
Glass products (000. tons)	77	31.2	15.6	53.2	93	21.5	21.5	57.0	65.6	24.4	30.9	44.7	67	22.4	32.8	44.8

(*continued*)

Table 4.10 Major Industrial Products, 1995–98 (continued)

Products	1995				1996				1997				1998			
	Total	Share in Total (%)			Total	Share in Total (%)			Total	Share in Total (%)			Total	Share in Total (%)		
		SOEs	Private	FIPs		SOEs	Private	FIPs		SOEs	Private	FIPs		SOEs	Private	FIPs
Steel (000. tons)	470	84.7	2.1	13.2	868	57.9	1.7	40.3	978	49.7	0.8	49.5	853.1	56.1	1.1	42.9
Transformers (piece)	6,186	79.8	0.0	20.2	6,910	74.3	0.0	25.7	6,549	80.6	0.0	19.4	4525	68.3	0.0	31.7
Televisions (000. pieces)	770	78.8	3.6	17.5	741	63.2	5.8	31.0	533	31.2	2.5	66.3	538	29.6	2.8	67.7
Automobiles (piece)	3,524	0.0	0.0	100.0	5,806	0.0	0.0	100.0	6,535	0.0	0.0	100.0	6,404	0.0	0.0	100.0
Monosodium Glutamate (000. tons)	65	0.0	0.0	100.0	87	0.0	0.0	100.0	91	0.0	0.0	100.0	105	0.0	0.0	100.0

Source: GSO 1999b, pp. 214–24.

An examination of the share of FIPs in GDP provides a better result. The share of FIPs in GDP increased from 2 percent in 1992 to 3.6 percent in 1994, 6.7 percent in 1995 and 9.1 percent in 1998. The FIPs have remained at the highest economic growth rate among all economic sectors in Vietnam, with an annual growth rate of around 20 percent for 1996 and 1997, and reducing to 16.9 percent for 1998 (GSO 1999b, pp. 25–6). Based on the data on the share of the FDI sector in GDP, the direct contribution of FIPs to GDP growth has been estimated as shown in Table 4.9. Except for 1994, the average contribution of FIPs to GDP growth has been between 1 percent to 1.5 percent, just lower than that of the state and household sectors. Such contributions would be very significant if bearing in mind the fact that the FDI-related sector is much smaller than the state and household sectors.

The contribution of FDI flows to economic growth can also be seen in the contribution of FDI to creating new industries or significantly increasing the output of existing industries. As shown in Table 4.10, in 1998 FIPs produced 100 percent of the output of crude oil, automobiles and monosodium glutamate, 67 percent of television, 44.8 percent of glass production, 42.9 percent of steel and 40.7 percent of garments. In other industries such as canned fruit, vegetable oil or transformer production, FIPs also accounted for more than 30 percent of the total output.

Another way to examine the contribution of FDI flows to GDP growth is to look at the performance of FIPs in the sense that the better the performance of FIPs, the higher the contribution of FDI flows to GDP growth. In general, the performance of FIPs has been low with only one-third of operating FIPs making a profit in the period under review. Only 40 percent of FIPs in food processing, garment, footwear, telecommunication, construction, and apartment rental, and 20 percent of FIPs in agriculture, fishery, forestry and hotel and the development of infrastructure of industrial zones are profitable (Phan 1998, pp. 9–10). While data on the performance of FIPs for the whole period 1988–98 are not available, the survey of FIPs in 1996 shows that the number of inefficient FIPs had increased from 197 in 1994 to 317 in 1995, and to 342 for the first 6 months of 1996. The losses hence increased from 54.3 million in 1994 to $133.7 million in 1995, and $96 million for the first 6 months of 1996 (GSO 1998, pp. 544–51). The low efficiency of many FIPs has lowered the contribution of FDI to GDP growth.

There have been several reasons for the inefficient performance of FIPs, such as poor physical and economic infrastructure or the 'strategic losses' tactic that foreign investors have been accused of applying to force local partners to quit joint ventures. However, the low level of production capacity utilization is also another reason that has led to the losses. FIPs have recorded the highest percentage of enterprises which utilized less than 50 percent of their production capacity in the 1997 industrial survey. The number of FIPs that achieved from 50 percent to 95 percent of production capacity was also lower than that of domestic enterprises. Such low levels are attributed to the fact that many FIPs were still in the early stage of their operation and still needed some time to accelerate production. The results of the 1995 economic survey and the 1998 industrial survey also showed that the turnover–capital ratio of FIEs in manufacturing sector had increased from 0.45 in 1994 to 0.52 in 1997, while the ratio reduced from 1.29 to 0.81 for the whole sector (GSO 1999 b, c).

The regression analysis in the following chapter will show that the performance of FIEs has a statistically significant positive correlation with the duration of their operation in Vietnam.

In short, while many FIPs have been making losses, the contribution of FDI flows to GDP growth has been very important, accounting for between 1 to 1.5 percentage points of GDP growth annually. Moreover, FDI flows have also created many new industries or increased the output of many others. The low efficiency of FIPs, however can be attributed to the low level of production capacity utilization, as many of them had just started their production.

Conclusion

This chapter has examined the macroeconomic impact of FDI flows on the economy of Vietnam. In general, FDI flows have contributed to covering the savings–investment gap by directly providing investment capital or indirectly promoting and encouraging domestic savings. In some industries, FDI flows have even competed with local industries, but such negative effects are not significant.

FDI flows also increase the exports of the whole country by providing modern technology and access to international markets. Even FIPs require large imports of machinery, equipment and materials and have generated a trade deficit, but this has reduced recently. FIPs also contribute to government revenue through several forms of tax, and such contributions will become more significant in the future. By contributing to covering the savings–investment, foreign exchange and fiscal gaps, FDI flows have contributed to promoting GDP growth of between 1 to 1.5 percentage point annually.

The government of Vietnam has played a decisive role in making use of FDI flows by introducing several tax incentives to encourage them to manufacturing sectors that will, in turn, create important backward effects for the whole economy; by limiting the direct competition with local enterprises; and by minimizing the outflows of dividends on foreign contributions by encouraging reinvestment in Vietnam. In general, the government of Vietnam has promoted the positive impacts and minimized the detrimental effects of FDI flows, and hence made FDI flows a very important investment source for socio-economic development in Vietnam. In this regard, the government has made FDI flows an important, rather than a substitute, source of capital for development. Foreign direct investment brings into Vietnam modern technology and management skills, and promotes the industrialization process.

Notes

[1] A backward linkage is the increase in demand of the inputs (such as raw materials) for FDI projects.

[2] For local firms' loans, the interest rates would normally be 2 percent higher than LIBOR.

5
Foreign Direct Investment and the Industrialization Process in Vietnam

This chapter analyzes the role of FDI flows in transferring modern technology, know-how and management skills, in promoting the government's dual strategy of export-oriented industrialization and import-substitution industrialization. Following on from this, this chapter analyzes the government policies that have influenced the contributions of FDI to Vietnam's industrialization. Several regression analyses will be used to support the finding that government policies have been important to the positive impact of FDI flows on Vietnam's industrialization.

Technology transfer

The 1986 socio-economic reforms aimed to mobilize local as well as foreign capital, technology and management skills to promote industrialization in Vietnam. Foreign investment was seen as a major potential source of updated technology and skills to replace old and obsolete technologies and hence to promote the industrialization and modernization of Vietnam.

A greater part of technology used in Vietnam is obsolete. Machinery and equipment that are still being used in many enterprises are between two to five generations out of date (Thu 1997 cited in Bezanson et al. 1999, p. 63). The technologies and equipment used in many state-owned enterprises (SOEs) that receive extensive financial support from the government have also been in very poor condition. Several surveys have revealed that only 18 percent of SOEs have been equipped with new technology, and such new technology has been introduced only since 1986. A survey of 200 SOEs in 1997 conducted by the Central Institute of Economic Management in co-operation with Japan's Overseas Economic Co-operation Fund also found that one of the three most serious difficulties for the development of SOEs is outdated technology and equipment (Hagiu et al. 1998, p. 165). About 82 percent of SOEs still use technology that is between two to four generations older than in other countries. Some SOEs still use equipment manufactured in 1939, or even earlier (Nguyen et al. 1996, pp. 24–5).

Given the circumstances, foreign direct investment is understandably considered as a major source of modern technology for Vietnam, and several government policies have been issued to promote the technology transfer process.

Foreign investment and technology transfer

In general, newer technology has been brought into Vietnam with FDI flows since 1988 and has contributed to the production of several new products or improved the production of existing products that better satisfy domestic and export demand. The products of foreign invested enterprises (FIEs) at least meet Vietnam's quality standards and some products meet international standards.

The Law on Foreign Direct Investment in Vietnam requires that modern technology transfer under FDI must be:

- technology that creates new and essential products in Vietnam or products for export;
- technology that improves technical capability, product quality and production capacity; and/or
- technology that saves materials and energy; that exploits and utilizes natural resources effectively (NPPH 1999, p. 41).

Between 1988 and 1998, 219 foreign invested projects (or about 10 percent of the total) were registered as including technology transfers, accounting for around 10 percent of the total FIPs.

Those projects have been mainly in the manufacturing sector with 128 projects (accounting for 58.4 percent) while only 71 projects were in the service sector and 20 projects in the primary sector. In the manufacturing sector, labour-intensive industries (including food, beverages, textiles, garments, leather goods and wood products) account for 44 projects, while capital-intensive industries account for 84 projects that were involved in the technology transfer process. The heavy concentration of technology transfer projects in the manufacturing sector has coincided with the general trend of FDI in that sector in Vietnam. Moreover, the high percentage of capital intensive industries in total technology transfer projects and the lower share for export-oriented industries illustrate Vietnam's comparative advantage of cheap labour and the government's policies to promote the development of infant supportive import-substitution industries.

Joint ventures dominated technology transfer with 128 projects, or 58.4 percent of the total. On the other hand, the 100 percent foreign-owned ventures account for only 33.5 percent while business cooperation contract (BCC) ventures account for 8.2 percent. This reflects the fact that until recently, joint ventures were still the dominant form of FDI in Vietnam. In terms of country of origin, the Asian Newly Industrializing Countries (NICs) and Association of Southeast Asian Nations (ASEAN) countries are the major sources of technology transfer to Vietnam under FDI, accounting for 58.9 percent of total projects. Of the developed countries, those of the European Union account for 11.4 percent, Japan accounts for 8.2 percent while the United States and Canada account for 5 percent. This trend reflects the fact that ASEAN and the Asian NICs are the major foreign investors in Vietnam while FDI flows from the United States, Japan have flowed to Vietnam in large amounts only since 1995.

In general, FDI flows have brought with them modern and better technology compared to that used by local enterprises. This situation has been illustrated in the industrial sector that received over 63.4 percent of FDI flows between 1988 and 1998. In fact, FIEs have been using more modern machinery and equipment, and generating higher productivity as shown in Table 5.1. The data collected from the 1995 economic survey and the 1998 industrial survey revealed that FIEs had higher levels of fixed assets per enterprise, higher fixed assets per employee and higher total capital per employee than those of SOEs or private enterprises for both 1995 and 1998 (GSO 1998; 1999b, 1999c). The ratio of fixed assets over capital for FIEs was also higher than that of SOEs and private enterprises for both 1995 and 1998. Those indices show that FIEs have been capital-intensive, using more expensive machinery and equipment,[1] and hence were more likely to have used more modern technology. The gap between SOEs and FIEs in terms of fixed assets per employee and total capital per employee was reduced between 1995 and 1998 but widened between FIEs and private enterprises over the same period due to government attempts to reorganize and restructure the SOEs, and the rapid growth of the private sector as well as the less capital-intensive nature of private enterprises in Vietnam.

In addition, the data in Table 5.1 show that the FIEs also generated higher productivity compared to local enterprises as the level of turnover per employee for FIEs is twice that of SOEs and private enterprises for both 1995 and 1998. The reduction of level of turnover per employee between 1995 and 1998 for FIEs, SOEs and private enterprises, however, reflects the effects of the regional economic crisis on the Vietnamese economy. The capital-intensive nature of FIEs, on the other hand, made their ratio of turnover over total capital the lowest compared to SOEs and private enterprises, though this ratio increased from 43.6 percent in 1995 to 58.6 percent in 1998 (GSO 1998; 1999b, 1999c).

TABLE 5.1 Major Indicators of Vietnam's Industry, 1995–98

	1995			1998		
	SOEs	Private enterprise	FIEs	SOEs	Private enterprise	FIEs
Net fixed assets/capital (%)	64	49.6	78	34.7	44.7	64.5
Fixed asset per firm (VND bill.)	13	0.4	53.3	24.4	0.013	93.7
Fixed assets per employee (VND bill.)	0.05	0.018	0.377	0.06	0.004	0.321
Total capital per employee[a] (VND bill.)	0.079	0.036	0.483	0.172	0.009	0.5
Turnover per employee[b] (VND bill.)	0.121	0.088	0.211	0.093	0.02	0.2
Turnover/total capital[c] (%)	153.4	242.6	43.6	80	310	58.6

Note: [a] Data on 1995 capital are as at 1 January 1995.
[b] 1998's turnover per employee is at 1994 prices.
[c] 1998's turnover is converted from 1998's turnover at 1994 prices by using GDP deflators.
Source: GSO 1998; 1999b, 1999c.

The introduction of modern technology in FIEs can also be seen in their level of automation of production lines, age of equipment and the introduction of waste processing systems.

The production lines of FIEs are mostly fully or partly automated or fully mechanical, and only a small number of production lines are partly mechanical or manual. On the other hand, the number of production lines of SOEs and private enterprises classified as fully automated is low compared to FIEs. For SOEs, the majority is partly automated, fully mechanical or partly mechanical, while those of private enterprises are mainly fully, or partly, mechanical and manual. Of the FIEs, the joint venture form, especially joint ventures with SOEs, seem to use more modern technology (GSO 1999c, p. 64).

However, the technological superiority of FIEs is not demonstrable in terms of the age of equipment. In general, the majority of FIEs (95.8 percent) used equipment and machinery that was less than 20 years old compared to 83.9 percent for SOEs and 95.2 percent for private enterprises. However, private enterprises had the largest percentage of enterprises using machinery and equipment less than 10 years old as many of them were established after 1986. In contrast, only 59.2 percent of FIEs used machinery and equipment less than 10 years old (GSO 1999c, pp. 88–90).

Another index that demonstrates the high level of technology used in FIEs is the level of waste processing systems introduced in FIEs. In 1998, 53.9 percent of FIEs had introduced waste processing systems compared to 44 percent for SOEs and 36.1 percent for private enterprises (GSO 1999c, pp. 65–7).

In short, the examination of several indices of FIEs, SOEs and private enterprises, such as fixed assets per employee, turnover per employee, fixed assets over total capital, level of automation of production lines, lifetime of equipment and the capacity of waste processing systems, has shown that FIEs have used more modern technology and equipment, generating higher productivity compared to local enterprises. In other words, FDI flows have brought into Vietnam relatively modern technology and equipment needed to promote the country's industrialization and modernization.

In addition to introducing modern machinery and equipment, foreign investors also transfer modern technology to Vietnam through local staff and employee training and by bringing foreign experts to Vietnam. For instance, 100 percent of textile/garment firms and 90 percent of electronic firms surveyed used their co-operation with foreign partners to obtain modern technology, modern management and marketing skills by sending Vietnamese employees for training overseas or receiving advice from foreign experts attached to the firms (Tran 1999a).

In another example, in a joint venture to produce television picture tubes worth $170 million between Hanoi Electronic Co. (HANEL) and Orion Electronics Co. (a subsidiary of Daewoo), 72 engineers and technicians as well as several workers were sent to Korea for training in the production of television picture tubes, technology handling, assembly tubes or production management and about 20 Korean engineers helped set the project up (Tran 1999a, p. 215). Another example is the business co-operation contract between Vietnam Post and Telecommunication and Australia's TELSTRA, where 2,000 Vietnamese staff have been trained either in Vietnam, in Australia or in third countries to obtain modern technological know-how (VIR 1997).

The level of technology transferred through FDI flows, however, has varied among industries. Advanced technology has been transferred in the oil and gas industries, telecommunications, cement, electronic, automobile industries and some processing industries (such as banana and mushroom processing, and vegetable production by using advanced biological technology). Thanks to modern technology brought in by foreign investors, Vietnam has been able to produce several kinds of modern telecommunications equipment such as switchboards, optic fibre cables and hence improve the quality of telecommunication services within a short period. Ordinary technology has been transferred in mechanical, metallurgy, chemical, light industries and some food processing industries. Old and obsolete technology has been transferred in some projects in the areas of mineral resources exploitation, animal feed production, and footwear industries.

While technology transferred through FDI flows has been considered modern, equal to, or better than, advanced technology that has been used by local enterprises, such transferred technology has been mainly labour-intensive, simple assembly and equal to only the median level of technology that has been used in other countries in the region (VNN 1999). This has been attributed to the fact that the majority of foreign investors in Vietnam are small and medium corporations from ASEAN or the Asian NICs, which themselves have not had access to the latest technology. Moreover, as 40 percent of equipment and machinery imported into Vietnam for FIEs is still over 10 years old, this has limited the transfer of advanced technology.

On the other hand, cheap local labour and low incomes also limit the opportunity to introduce modern technology. Such a conclusion on the nature of transferred technology is supported by regression analyses in the following sections, where it is shown that modern technology has not played a decisive role in determining the exports and profit level of FIEs.

Problems associated with technology transfer

Besides bringing modern technology, know-how, equipment and management skills to Vietnam, the technology transfer process under FDI has also generated several accompanying problems, namely transfer pricing and the importation of old technology and equipment.

The problem of transfer pricing occurs when foreign investors overstate the prices of imported machinery, equipment and technology. By overstating these prices, foreign investors will increase their share in a project's legal capital and hence increase their share in the project's profit and avoid paying high tax. In several cases, those prices are 10–20 percent higher than the world's market prices (Nguyen 1996).

Another investigation of 12 FIEs in 1995 by the Swiss quality control firm, SGS, also found a transfer pricing problem in 6 FIEs with overpricing of $14 million. On average, the prices had been inflated 1.4 times. A typical example is the BGI Tien Giang Brewery joint venture, where the cost of the project was inflated by $9.1 million (Nguyen 1995).

Another problem associated with technology transfer under FDI flows is the importation of old machinery and equipment and, therefore, old technology in some sectors. The importation of second-hand machinery and equipment happened mainly in mineral exploitation, food processing, animal feed production and shoe-making. An examination of 727 equipment and 3 production lines in 42 FIEs has revealed that 60–70 percent of the equipment was second hand, and some of it had been made as long ago as 1929 (Nguyen 1996).

Major causes of transfer pricing problems and the importation of obsolete equipment and technology are the lack of information, experience and knowledge of Vietnamese partners. As a consequence, they leave foreign partners to decide on the importation of machinery, equipment and technology for the joint ventures. Another reason is the lack of government control over the technology transferring process. While the regulations require that any kind of technology transfer (including transfer of know-how, technical information and training.) needs to be done through a contract, and is subject to government approval in order to avoid the transfer of inappropriate technology or equipment, in reality this has happened in around only two-thirds of FDI projects. Only 94 contracts have been submitted for approval. Therefore, where the foreign investors are dishonest and there is a lack of government supervision, problems of transfer pricing and the importation of old technology and equipment can easily occur.

In short, while technology transferred to Vietnam through FDI flows has been considered as equal to the medium level of technology used in other countries in the region, the problems of transfer pricing and the importation of old technology have reduced the the desired outcome of rapid infusions of up-to-date technology.

Policies on technology transfer

The relatively modern technology transferred to Vietnam under FDI flows, and the contribution of technology transferred in the manufacturing sector—especially in developing import-substitution industries—have been attributed to favourable government policies. Considering FDI as an important source of modern technology, know-how and management skills, the government of Vietnam has given tax incentives to projects that include technology transfer. Foreign Direct Investment projects that use advanced technology or invest in research and development will enjoy a profit tax of 20 percent (compared to 25 percent for ordinary projects), a one-year profit tax exemption, and a two-year profit tax deduction of 50 percent after the projects start making profits. For projects that include technology transfer and also belong to the special priority investment list (such as producing new and rare materials, using bio-technology and electronic technology, new technology to produce telecommunications equipment or information technology), the tax exemption period is increased to four years. Moreover, tax incentives of 10 percent profit tax and a tax exemption of eight years after projects have started making a profit are offered for FDI projects that use modern technology invested in high-technology zones established by the government (NPPH 1999).

While promoting the transfer of modern technology and equipment, the government of Vietnam also discourages the transfer of technology that generates detrimental effects on the environment, work safety, people's health, national defence, security and culture.

Realizing the potential problems of transfer pricing, the government has required that the value of transferred technology, while still subject to agreement between the concerned parties, would not be beyond the following:

- 0–5 percent of the sale price of related products during the technology transfer period;
- 0–25 percent of the after-tax profit earned from the sale of related products or service during the technology transfer period;
- 0–8 percent of the total invested capital in the case where technology has been used as the legal capital contribution; or
- 20 percent of legal capital in the case where technology has been used as the legal capital contribution and the time for technology transfer would not be longer than 7 years (VIR 1998b; NPPH 1999).

In conclusion, FDI flows to Vietnam since 1988 have brought with them modern technology, contributed to produce new products or improved the quality of existing products and in general, generated higher productivity. Several tax incentives have been given in order to promote such technology transfer process. However, due to the inexperience of the Vietnamese partners, problems such as transfer pricing, importation of old equipment and technology have occurred and require closer government scrutiny.

Vietnam's industrialization

This and the following sections examine how FDI has contributed to the industrialization process in Vietnam and the government's dual industrialization strategy of promoting the development of both export-oriented industries and import-substitution industries. In particular, the contribution of FDI in making use of the country's comparative advantages to produce export products as well as contributing to the establishment of infant import-substitution industries will be analyzed. Several regression analyses will be used to determine the impact of government policies on maximizing the contribution of FDI.

Vietnam's industrialization started in 1975 when the country was reunited, with the main priority being given to the development of heavy industries. This industrialization process accelerated after the socio-economic reforms of 1986 and more attention has been given to the development of export-oriented industries. As shown in Table 5.2, the share of industrial and service sectors in both Vietnam's gross domestic product (GDP) and total output increased, while the share of agriculture in GDP decreased, from 40.7 percent in 1990 to 23.6 percent in 1998, and from 35 percent to 26 percent in total output for the same period. In particular, the share of industry in GDP increased from 33.2 percent in 1990 to 40.8 percent in 1998. Industry also maintained a high and stable growth rate during the 1990s with an average growth rate of over 11 percent. The service sector, while remaining the largest share in GDP recorded unstable growth rates during the 1990s.

Such an accelerated growth of industrialization in Vietnam, especially the increasing share of the industrial sector in GDP as well as in total output, has been attributed to the government's dual industrialization strategy of promoting the development of both export-oriented and infant import-substitution industries. The major content of Vietnam's industrialization strategy that was set out by Vietnam's Communist Party's 8th Party Congress is to industrialize and modernize Vietnam by "establishing some key industries in the areas of food processing, oil and gas, electronics and informatics, biological technology, manufacturing and producing new material" (NPPH 1996, p. 179). Based on this dual industrialization strategy, priority is being given to developing the following industries:

TABLE 5.2 Vietnam's GDP and Output Structure, 1990–98 (percent)

	1990	1991	1992	1993	1994	1995	1996	1997	1998
GDP structure									
Industry share	18.6	19.3	20.4	21.2	21.9	22.5	23.4	24.5	25.9
Agriculture share	40.7	39.2	38.6	37.1	35.5	26.2	25.1	24.2	23.6
Service share	40.7	41.5	41.0	41.7	42.6	51.3	51.5	51.3	50.5
Output structure									
Industry share	33.2	34.9	36.0	36.4	36.5	35.8	37.1	39.0	40.8
Agriculture share	35.0	34.3	32.7	31.3	28.9	28.5	27.2	26.8	26.0
Service share	31.8	30.8	31.3	32.3	34.6	35.7	35.7	34.2	33.2
Growth rate									
Industrial growth rate	2.5	9.9	14.6	12.1	12.9	13.2	14.2	13.8	12.1
Agricultural growth rate	1.5	2.2	7.3	3.8	3.9	4.4	4.4	4.7	3.4
Service growth rate	10.2	7.6	7.1	10.1	11.1	19.6	9.9	7.8	4.0

Source: GSO 1996, 1999b, 1999c.

- export-oriented industries such as food processing, garments, leather products, and electronics, making use of Vietnam's comparative advantages of cheap labour and abundant natural resources;
- basic supportive industries that will promote and facilitate the development of other industries and create strong export-oriented industries; and
- new industries that will maintain Vietnam's comparative advantages in the future such as mechanical and electronic industries, chemical and petrochemical industries (Ishikawa 1998a, p. 9).

This dual strategy resembles those of Japan, South Korea, and Taiwan in their early stages of industrialization when the development of infant import-substitution industries created favourable conditions for the development of export-oriented industries.

The government of Vietnam considers foreign investment sources, especially in the form of FDI, as an important additional source of investment capital, foreign exchange and modern technology needed for accelerating industrialization. Accordingly, several government policies have been issued to promote FDI to support Vietnam's dual industrialization strategy. Tax incentives—including low profit taxes and tax exemptions and deductions—local market protection, and foreign currency balancing support have been given to FDI projects that contribute to the development of either export-oriented industries or import-substitution industries. As a result of those policies, large amounts of FDI have flowed into the industrial sector and contributed significantly to high industrial growth as well as increased the share of the industrial sector in GDP and total output.

While the data on FIEs' contribution to the industrial share of GDP are not available, the data on the contribution of FIEs to industrial output in Table 5.3 show that FIEs have accounted for an important share in both industrial capital and output. In terms of the share of FIEs in industrial capital, this increased from 41.3 percent of total industrial capital at the beginning of 1995 to 44.7 percent in 1998. Also, the share of FIEs in industrial output increased from 20 percent in 1994 to 31.8 percent in 1998. FIEs achieved high growth rates of over 50 percent in 1995 and over 20 percent for the 1996–98 period, many times higher than that of SOEs or the private sector.

As FIEs account for about one-third of total industrial output and recorded high growth rates, they have been considered important in promoting industrial growth and increasing the industrial share in GDP and total output. The data in Table 5.3 show that, except for 1996, FIEs accounted for about half of total industrial growth in Vietnam over the

TABLE 5.3 Structure of Vietnam's Industrial Output and Capital, 1994–98 (percent)

	Capital	Output	Output growth rate	Contribution to growth*
1994 SOEs	52.8	68.1	n.a.	n.a.
Private	5.9	11.9	n.a.	n.a.
FIEs	41.3	20.0	n.a.	n.a.
1995 SOEs	n.a.	50.3	–10.8	–7.3
Private	n.a.	24.6	14.9	17.8
FIEs	n.a.	25.1	51.8	10.3
1996 SOEs	n.a.	49.3	11.9	6.0
Private	n.a.	24.0	11.5	2.8
FIEs	n.a.	26.7	21.7	5.4
1997 SOEs	n.a.	48.0	10.8	5.3
Private	n.a.	23.1	9.5	2.3
FIEs	n.a.	28.9	23.2	6.2
1998 SOEs	47.5	46.2	7.9	3.8
Private	7.9	22.0	6.7	1.5
FIEs	44.7	31.8	23.3	6.7

* Calculated based on the formula in Table 4.9.
Source: GSO 1999b.

1994–98 period. In other words, FIEs are the main driving force for industrial growth in Vietnam.

Figure 5.1 also shows that in some industrial sectors like minerals, motor vehicles, leather or electronics, FIEs were the major source of growth over 1994–98 period.

In conclusion, the development of both export-oriented and infant import-substitution industries accelerated during the 1990s. The share of industry in GDP and in total output increased significantly while the growth rate of industrial output remained at a relatively high level during the 1990s. The FDI flows, through the performance of FIEs, have contributed significantly to such development.

The development of export-oriented industries

This section examines how FDI flows make use of the comparative advantages of Vietnam to produce export products. In addition, government policies to attract FDI flows to develop export-oriented industries will be reviewed. A regression analysis will be used to investigate the importance of government policies in creating a

Figure 5.1 Contribution to Industrial Growth in Major Industries, 1994–98

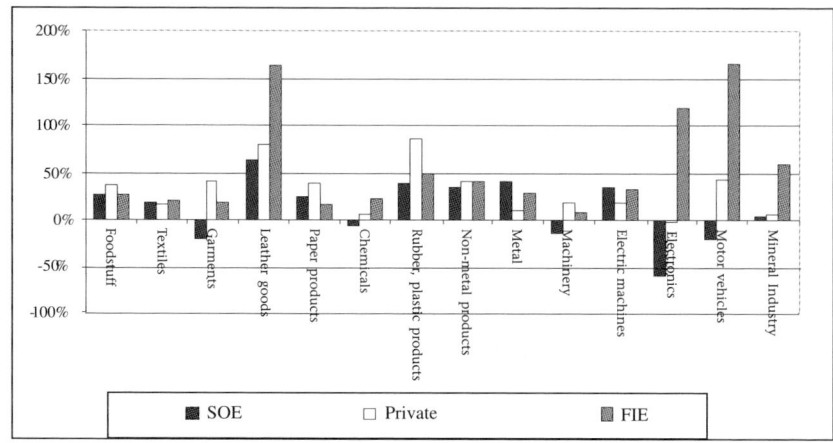

Source: GSO 1996; 1999 b.

favourable environment for the promotion of FIEs' export performance.

FDI's contribution to the development of export-oriented industries

As mentioned in Chapter 3, the exports of Vietnam increased significantly after the 1986 reforms. One of the main purposes of the reforms was to attract FDI to increase Vietnam's exports and increase the value-added component of these exports by using foreign capital, technology, and expertise as well as access to foreign markets to make use of Vietnam's comparative advantages.

However, the data show that FDI flows to Vietnam over the 1988–98 period were not focused on the industries in which Vietnam has comparative advantage (Table 5.4). Vietnam has comparative advantages in agricultural products such as rice, fish and eggs; mineral products such as crude oil, coke briquettes; and processing products such as coffee, tea, or garments. On the other hand, Vietnam does not have comparative advantages in producing capital-intensive products such as chemicals, machinery, metal and non-metal products or electric and electronic products.

Table 5.4 shows that of the total FDI commitment in manufacturing and primary sectors during 1988–98, only 20 percent went to the food, drink and tobacco industries; 6.5 percent to the garment industry; 3 percent to raw material production; and 6.6 percent to mineral industries. In contrast, 63.8 percent of committed FDI went to other

Table 5.4 Sectoral Revealed Comparative Advantages and Foreign Direct Investment Flows (percent)

	Share in total comm. FDI 1991–98	Share in total implemented FDI 1991–98	Share in implemented FDI							
			1991	1992	1993	1994	1995	1996	1997	1998
Mineral raw materials (incl. crude oil)	6.6	24.07	47.8	57.2	30.8	38.7	28.2	19.2	10.9	24.4
Raw materials	3.0	1.82	12.8	2.2	1.4	1.4	1.3	2.0	2.2	1.0
Food, foodstuffs, drinks, tobacco	20.1	14.96	4.3	13.0	29.8	10.7	17.1	8.7	17.0	15.7
Garments	6.5	6.62	10.1	4.5	5.5	4.7	7.4	9.3	8.2	1.9
Textiles	6.3	4.44	0.4	0.6	4.2	1.5	3.1	5.3	8.7	1.1
Leather goods	0.1	0.06	0.2	0.0	0.0	0.0	0.0	0.0	0.1	0.2
Wood, bamboo, furniture	0.4	0.59	3.5	2.1	1.2	0.7	1.1	0.3	0.3	0.1
Paper products	0.6	0.37	0.1	0.7	0.5	0.1	0.3	0.4	0.4	0.4
Coke, oil products	1.7	0.26	1.0	2.5	0.2	0.1	0.0	0.0	0.2	0.8
Chemicals and chemical products	10.4	7.34	0.9	1.1	3.8	2.0	3.8	11.1	6.6	17.1
Rubber, plastic products	1.8	1.51	0.9	3.1	1.5	1.1	1.6	1.0	1.7	1.8
Non-metal products	12.3	10.83	0.4	0.7	8.1	5.8	7.4	16.4	15.8	7.6
Metal	0.2	0.23	0.0	0.0	0.0	0.3	0.1	0.0	0.6	0.0
Metal products	4.1	4.55	0.3	0.0	1.4	7.8	6.7	1.5	4.7	4.8
Machinery and equipment	8.7	7.48	2.8	4.4	3.3	11.6	6.8	8.6	6.7	6.6
Electric and electronic machines and equipment	8.0	6.58	2.1	1.4	2.3	10.7	5.6	8.0	5.6	6.5
Transport equipment	7.9	7.37	11.7	6.2	5.7	2.4	8.2	7.7	8.9	8.8
Other manufactured goods	1.3	0.93	0.8	0.3	0.5	0.5	1.3	0.6	1.1	1.3

Source: GSO 1999a, 1999b, 1999c; MPDF 1999a, 1999b.

capital-intensive import-substitution industries. However, the data on implemented FDI show a different trend. Over 51 percent of total implemented FDI during 1988–98 was channelled to industries that Vietnam has a high revealed comparative advantage such foods, foodstuff, drink and tobacco, textile, garments, minerals, and raw materials, and less than 49 percent was channelled to capital-intensive industries. Notably, 24 percent of implemented FDI has gone to the mineral industry, mainly the oil and gas industry.

Though the actual FDI flows to export-oriented industries of Vietnam during the 1988–1998 period account for only half of the total FDI flows, their contribution to promoting the development of export-oriented industries was significant. As mentioned in chapter 4 (Table 4.7) the export volume of FIPs increased from a mere $52 million in 1991 to $2.6 billion in 1999 and the share of FIPs' exports in total exports also increased from 2.5 percent in 1991 to 24.2 percent in 1999. Moreover, the growth rate of FIPs exports remains at a high level while the country's export growth rate has fluctuated as a consequence of the regional financial crisis.

While FIPs have generated exports in all sectors, exports generated by FIEs in the mineral and industrial sectors have been the most important, accounting for over 90 percent of the total exports generated by FDI flows. A closer examination of the export performance of FIEs in mineral and industrial sectors reveals several interesting points.

The share of FIEs output in industries in which Vietnam has a comparative advantage and has exported a large percentage of output also increased rapidly between 1994 and 1998. Except for the oil and gas industry, where FIEs played a dominant role throughout the 1990s, the share of FIEs' output in garments, leather goods, office machines, furniture and mineral industries increased significantly. In the case of the garment industry, Vietnam's most rapid growing export-oriented industry during the 1990s, the share of FIEs' output increased from 11.5 percent of total garment output in 1994 to 21.4 percent in 1998. Moreover, the inflows of FDI to capital-intensive industries like electrical goods and electronics also create new export products that make use of Vietnam's cheap and educated labour.

Compared to local enterprises, FIEs have achieved a higher ratio of exports over total turnover. For the 1988–98 period, 528 FDI projects were registered to export part of their output, of which 335 projects exported 80–100 percent of output, 103 projects exported between 50–80 percent of output, and 90 projects exported less than 50 percent of their output. The 1998 industrial survey also revealed that in 1997, FIEs (especially 100 percent foreign-owned enterprises and joint ventures with both the state sector and non-state sector) recorded the highest ratios of exports over turnover of over 70 percent and over 55 percent for joint ventures with the state sector. With foreign connections and access to international markets, FIEs have performed better in comparison to local enterprises in terms of international market penetration. At least 40 percent of FIEs have exported their products, and the number of FIEs classified as unable to export has been very low, at around 10–15 percent compared to an average of 62.5 percent for the whole of Vietnam's industrial enterprises.

The export structure of FIEs shows an interesting trend over the 1990–98 period. Over that period, labour-intensive export products such as garments, textiles, food, wood and furniture were the major exports of FIEs. Moreover, the FDI flows have created new export products of electrical and electronic apparatus and appliances. Exports of new labour-intensive electrical and electronic apparatus and appliances (such as home audio and video equipment, electronic accessories and transformers) increased along with their share of total FIEs exports (from zero in 1992 to 41.2 percent in 1998), while the ratio of exports over turnover was as high as 67.3 percent for the whole 1991–98 period.

A typical example of these new labour intensive export electronic products are from Fujitsu's 100 percent foreign-owned project. Fujitsu established two factories to produce printed circuit board assemblies for computers in 1995 and has reached an average output of 1.5 million units per year. All Fujitsu's products in Vietnam are exported to its factories around the world, especially in Japan, Thailand and the Philippines. The export volume of the project has increased steadily from $47 million in 1996 to $279 million in 1997, $395 million in 1998 and was expected to have reached $1 billion in 2000 (Nguyen 1999c). Another example are the home electronic appliances produced by the joint venture between Daewoo and Hanoi Electronics Co. (HANEL). The Daewoo-HANEL joint venture has exported altogether more than 100,000 colour television sets to East Asia and the Middle East. Television picture tubes produced by another joint venture between Orion (a subsidiary of Daewoo) and HANEL have also been exported in large quantities. Of the 1.6 million picture tubes produced in 1997, 1 million were exported (UNIDO and DSI 1999, p. 139).

Most of the foreign investment in Vietnam from Japan and Asian NICs tends to be for export while foreign investment from the United States, Europe and ASEAN countries has focused on the domestic market. Between 1991 and 1998, the average ratio of exports over turnover of Asian NICs FDI projects was 48.1 percent, 44.8 percent for Japan FDI projects, 14.8 for FDI projects from the European Union and 11.8 percent for ASEAN FDI projects and 9.2 percent for FDI projects from the United States and Canada. When the exports of FDI projects have been broken down into sub-sectors, this pattern still remains. Except for the service sector, where the foreign currency earnings mainly come from domestic

84 *Foreign Direct Investment and Development in Vietnam*

activities, in manufacturing and primary sub-sectors, Asian NICs and Japan still record the highest ratio of exports over turnover. This high exports ratio of FDI projects from Japan and Asian NICs compared to the low ratio of FDI projects from the United States and European Union support the Kojima hypothesis[2] that Japanese FDI tends to be outward and export-orientated, focusing on using cheap labour in developing countries to produce export products. In contrast, FDI from the United States and the European Union tends to be inward, capital-intensive and focused on the local market (Kojima 1978, 1991).

In conclusion, while only half of actual FDI flows has been channelled to industries in which Vietnam has a comparative advantage, FDI flows have contributed significantly to promoting the development of export-oriented industries through FIEs. Moreover, FDI to import-substitution industries have also created new export products such as electronic appliances. Japan and Asian NICs FDI projects in Vietnam are export orientated while FDI projects from the United States and the European Union are inward oriented.

Government policies and the export performance of FIEs

Recognizing the importance of FIEs in promoting the development of export-oriented industries, the government has issued many policies to provide favourable conditions for FDI and FIEs that make use of Vietnam's comparative advantages of cheap labour and natural resources. Such policies could be classified into the three following groups:

- providing incentives to make FDI projects more profitable by offering tax incentives;
- providing a favourable environment to improve the performance of FIEs such as providing better infrastructure and reducing the costs of basic supplies; and
- providing a stable macroeconomic environment.

The government has provided tax incentives to attract FDI flows into export-oriented industries, in order to make use of Vietnam's comparative advantages of cheap labour and natural resources. There are two categories of FIEs that can enjoy government tax incentive. The first category is for FIEs that use large amounts of local labour or process agricultural products for export. Of this category, the FIEs that export over 50 percent of output will enjoy a reduced profit tax rate of 20 percent, a tax exemption for one year and a tax deduction of 50 percent for two years after the project starts making a profit. Other FIEs that export over 80 percent of output enjoy a reduced profit tax rate of 15 percent, a tax exemption for two years and a tax deduction of 50 percent for three years after the project starts making a profit. Moreover, FDI projects enjoy an import tax refund on materials imported to produce export products (NPPH 1999).

The second category is for other FIEs. Of this category, FIEs that export less than 50 percent of output will enjoy a reduced profit tax rate of 15 percent, and tax exemption for two years. FIEs that export between 50 percent and 80 percent of output will be given similar incentives, plus an additional two years of 50 percent tax deduction after the project starts making a profit. FIEs that export over 80 percent of output will enjoy a profit tax of 10 percent, two years' tax exemption, and two years' tax deduction of 50 percent (NPPH 1999).

In order to provide better infrastructure such as water and energy supply for FDI projects, especially export-oriented projects, the government has established several industrial and export processing zones and offers attractive tax incentives. For FIEs that specialize in producing export products, the profit tax of 10 percent and tax exemption of four years will be given if they invested in industrial and export processing zones. In general, the FDI projects located in industrial zones (IZs) and export processing zones (IPZs) have recorded higher ratios of exports over revenue. In 1998, for example, the FDI projects in IZs and IPZs achieved 52.8 percent of exports over revenue compared to 39.3 percent for all FDI projects.

Providing a stable macroeconomic environment and a competitive playing field for all enterprises is another aim of government policies. Since 1986, the government of Vietnam has maintained relatively stable macroeconomic conditions, despite the Asian regional economic crisis. The economy maintained a high growth rate for most of the time during the 1990s while inflation was kept under control. Furthermore, the government adjusted telephone, water and energy charges for FIEs in accordance with those for local enterprises. Moreover, there were several adjustment to the Law on Foreign Investment in Vietnam in 2000 in order to narrow the gap in treatment provided to local enterprises and FIEs. For instance, the FIEs can now use their rented land for collateral.

These government policies have created a favourable environment for the exports of FIEs and made them a major factor behind promoting the development of export-oriented industries. The regression analysis on the export performance of FIEs in three years 1996, 1997 and 1998 reveals the decisive role of government policies, especially tax incentives and domestic protection policies.

As mentioned in previous sections, the export performance of the FIEs in primary (mainly mining) industry and manufacturing sectors has been argued to be influenced by government tax policy, government domestic market protection policies, the share of foreign investors in FIEs' legal capital, the transfer of modern technology and the country of origin of foreign investors. It has been argued that the lower the tax ratio, the lower the domestic protection, the more technology transfer, the higher the export performance while FDI projects from Asian NICs and Japan seem to achieve better results in terms of export performance.

The full details of the regression analysis appear in Appendix 1. The main results of the regression analysis are as follows:

1996
ER96 = −0.017 − 0.249 PROTECT* + 0.144 FOREIGN − 0.369 TAX***
       (0.053)   (−1.9)   (1.11)   (−2.85)

       − 0.062 TECH + 0.302 COUNTRY**
       (−0.48)   (2.32)

$\bar{R}^2$ = 0.253   D-W = 2.1 $F_{(5,41)}$ = 4.112***   SE = 0.40   N = 47

1997
ER97 = 0.126 − 0.291 PROTECT*** + 0.088 FOREIGN − 0.195 TAX***
       (0.765)   (−4.08)   (1.2)   (−2.72)

       − 0.087 TECH + 0.227 COUNTRY***
       (−1.19)   (3.13)

$\bar{R}^2$ = 0.171   D-W = 2.09 $F_{(5,158)}$ = 7.71***   SE = 0.4   N = 164

1998
ER98 = −0.263* − 0.303 PROTECT*** + 0.269 FOREIGN*** − 0.257 TAX***
       (−1.89)   (−5.04)   (4.49)   (−4.2)

       − 0.175 TECH*** + 0.279 COUNTRY***
       (−2.9)   (4.6)

$\bar{R}^2$ = 0.308   D-W = 1.98 $F_{(5,189)}$ = 18.296***   SE = 0.35   N = 195
***, ** and * indicates significant at 1, 5 and 10 percent level respectively. The figures in brackets are t-statistics.
ER: Ratio of exports over revenue
PROTECT: Domestic market protection policies
FOREIGN: Foreign share in legal capital
TAX: Ratio of profit and revenue tax over revenue
TECH: Technology transfer
COUNTRY: Country of origin of foreign investors

The regression analysis on the export performance of FIEs in three years 1996, 1997 and 1998 shows the importance of government policies such as tax policies and domestic market protection policies on the export performance of FIEs. The major findings of this regression analysis are that the lower the tax rate, the higher the export performance of FIEs and the higher the domestic market protection, the lower the export performance. Moreover, as indicated, FDI flows from Japan and Asian NICs tend to be export-oriented.

In conclusion, FDI flows have played an important role in making use of Vietnam's comparative advantages of cheap labour and abundant natural resources to produce export products. The share of FIEs' output in the total output of those products increased significantly between 1994 and 1998. The regression analysis found that government policies, especially tax incentives and domestic market protection policies, played a decisive role in determining the export performance of FIEs. Other government interventions such as providing better infrastructure or a stable macroeconomic environment also contribute to facilitating the export performance of FIEs.

FDI and infant import-substitution industries

Another objective of Vietnam's dual industrialization strategy is to develop infant import-substitution industries to support the development of export-oriented industries as well as to maintain and create new advantages for Vietnam in the future. This section examines the arguments behind the development of such infant supportive import-substitution industries as well as the contribution of FDI and government.

The contribution of FDI

While the industrialization process in Vietnam started in 1975, the share of import-substitution industries in its industrial output has remained low. Before promulgating the Law on Foreign Investment at the end of 1987, the share of such import-substitution industries (including fuel, metallurgy, equipment and machinery production, electric and electronic, chemical, rubber and plastic, and metallic production industries) in the total industrial output has been as low as 27.6 percent in 1985, 27.8 percent in 1986, 28.1 percent in 1987 and 29.6 percent in 1988 (GSO 1996, p. 42). In addition, the machinery and equipment used in those industries are old and obsolete and hence the contribution of import-substitution industries to the support of export-oriented industries as well as the industrialization process has been small and insignificant. In other words, Vietnam has almost no infant supportive industries (Ishikawa 1998a, p. 7).

The major reasons for promoting the development of infant import-substitution industries is, therefore, to reduce the dependence on imports as well as reduce the trade deficit and promote the development of local industries to meet increasing domestic demand. A typical example is a government plan to promote the development of metallurgy industries in order to meet the increasing domestic demand for steel that stood at 1.3 million in 1996 and is projected to increase to 3.4 million tons in 2005 (Fukui 1998, pp. 38–9).

Another reason to promote the development of infant import-substitution industries is to create strong support industries to facilitate the development of export-oriented industries and create a firm foundation from which to move up the ladder of technology. The development of import-substitution industries will, in the long run, generate new comparative advantages, generate higher added value and therefore avoid dependence on cheap labour (Ishikawa 1998a, p. 15). During the 1990s, the underdevelopment of such import-substitution industries caused the export-oriented industries to develop based on exports of unprocessed or simply processed raw materials, or on sub-contractual bases.

In the case of the garment industry, its export value increased significantly from $67.7 million in 1986 to $1.5 billion in 1997 (GSO 1996, 1999b). But this increase was based on sub-contracts, where Vietnamese contractors made garments for export using foreign supplies of fabrics, designs and necessary materials. As the textile industry has grown more slowly than the garment industry, the fabrics needed to fulfil sub-contracts have been imported and, as a consequence, the high export earnings of the garment industry have been offset by the high cost of imported fabric, which increased from 33.2 million metres in 1986 to 414.3 million metres in 1997 (GSO 1996, 1999b; UNIDO and DSI 1999, p. 115). Moreover, the exports of garments based on sub-contracts and imported materials have led to a low value-added earning per worker for the garment industry, that stayed at $1,770 in 1998, compared to $7,980 in Malaysia and $15,560 in Singapore (UNIDO and DSI 1999, p. 115). This situation was also reproduced in other industries. Automobile, motorcycle, measurement instrument and electronic industries had to import materials which accounted for 70–95 percent of the products' value (Tran 1998, p. 25; UNIDO and DSI 1999, p. 137).

The international trend towards economic integration may be another factor that requires rapid development of infant import-substitution industries. Those industries will create a strong basis for Vietnam's industries to compete with foreign producers when Vietnam removes its tariff and non-tariff barriers as a requirement of joining trading blocs like the ASEAN free trade area (AFTA), the Asian Pacific Economic Co-operation (APEC) or the World Trade Organization. Based on those arguments, there is the need to develop the infant import-substitution industries in order to increase added value and reduce the dependence on imports of materials and machinery.

The infant supportive import-substitution industries in Vietnam are likely to be the following industries:

- automobile and parts
- iron and steel
- oil refining
- petrochemicals
- urea fertilizers
- cement (Ishikawa 1998b).

The promotion of such infant supportive import-substitution industries has been reflected in the list of priority investment projects, where the projects produce import-substitution products which account for a large share of the total industrial priority projects (Box 3).

FDI flows have been considered an important source for the development of these supportive import-substitution industries because the latter requires large amounts of investment capital and modern technology, Moreover, FDI is also seen as able to promote the development of such industries within a short period of time before Vietnam starts to reduce its tariff and non-tariff barriers in order to join trading blocs like AFTA. Since FDI started to flow into Vietnam in 1988, FDI has played a very important role in creating whole new infant industries (such as the oil and gas, oil refining and automotive industry) or expanding and modernizing existing ones (such as the metallurgy, chemical and cement industries).

In general, as mentioned in Chapter 3, the volume of FDI committed and implemented in those industries increased over the 1990s until 1997 when the Asian regional economic crisis led to the reduction in FDI flows to Vietnam. Table 5.5 shows that the contribution of FDI flows in the total capital stock of infant import-substitution industries[3] in Vietnam increased between 1994 and 1998. The total capital of FIEs in those industries increased from $468 million in 1994 to $3,087.4 million in 1998. The share of FIEs' capital in total capital of those industries also increased from 27.3 percent in 1994 to 57.3 percent in 1998, higher than the share of SOEs and private enterprises in the total capital. Of the $3.7 billion increase in the total capital of those industries between 1994 and 1998, the increase in FIEs' capital accounts for over 70 percent or, in other words, FDI flows were the major source of increasing the capital of infant import-substitution industries in Vietnam between 1994 and 1998. Such increases in capital have led to the increase in the share of FIEs' output in the total output of those infant import-substitution industries, though at a lower magnitude. Between 1994 and 1998, the share of FIEs in the total output of those industries almost doubled, and such increases in FIEs' output has explained 18.6 percent of the total increase in output of

> **Box 3**
> **Priority Industrial Investment Projects**
>
> 1. Exploration, exploitation and downstream processing of minerals;
> 2. Development of petrochemical industry;
> 3. Production of high quality steel, alloy, non-ferrous metal, special metal, billet and sponge iron for industries;
> 4. Manufacture of machine tools for metal machining;
> 5. Manufacture of spare parts for automobile and motorbike; manufacture and assembly of equipment, vehicle and machinery for construction;
> 6. Manufacture of diesel engines with advanced techniques and technology; manufacture of machinery and spare parts for engines and hydraulic and compressing machines;
> 7. Building of ships; and manufacture of equipment and spare parts for cargo ships and fishing boats;
> 8. Manufacture of equipment and component packs for oil and gas exploitation and energy mines; manufacture of large-size lifting equipment;
> 9. Manufacture of precision mechanical equipment; and jigs and die manufacturing;
> 10. Manufacture of equipment for treatment of waste water;
> 11. Manufacture of electrical middle and high voltage devices;
> 12. Production of special cement, composite materials, sound-insulating materials, electrical-insulating materials, heat-insulating materials and wood-substitute synthetic materials;
> 13. Production of silk; fibres of various kinds, textile products for exports, and special fabrics used in industries;
> 14. Production of high quality materials for production of footwear and garments for export;
> 15. Production of high quality packages for export [sic];
> 16. Production of medicines meeting the *GMP* international standards; and production of new pharmaceutical products by biotechnology.
>
> *Source*: NPPH 1999.

those industries. Moreover, the non-metal products industries (especially the cement industry) and radio, television and telecommunication equipment industries have achieved the highest growth rate of output of over 36 and 17 times respectively.

Not only do they generate high growth rates of output, but FDI also creates whole new industries such as oil and gas industries, petrochemical industries and automotive industries. For the automotive industries, eleven joint ventures with well-known car manufacturers from Japan, Germany,

TABLE 5.5 Foreign Invested Enterprises' Contribution to Total Industrial Capital and Output, 1994 and 1998 ($ million)

	1994 Capital			1994 Output			1998 Capital			1998 Output		
	Total	FIEs	Share	Total	FIEs	Share	Total	FIEs	Share	Total	FIEs	Share
Total	1,711.3	468	27.3	2,229.2	177.4	8.0	5,387.5	3,087.4	57.3	7,176.5	1,096.4	15.3
Coke, oil products and nuclear fuel	15.6	11.2	71.9	148.9	16	10.8	54.4	41.9	77.1	7.8	0	0
Chemicals and chemical products	277.7	42.6	15.4	577.8	26.1	4.5	654	296.2	45.3	710.5	152.9	21.5
Rubber, plastic products	83.6	20.5	24.5	133.1	6.6	4.9	388	186.7	48.1	365.7	73	20
Non-metal products	604.2	89.8	14.9	586.8	6.8	1.2	1,920.4	883.1	46	1,269.3	246.1	19.4
Metal	163.1	71.7	43.9	215.1	56.7	26.4	341.5	174.9	51.2	386.2	116.2	30.1
Metal products	69.3	19.5	28.1	80.8	9.7	12	431.2	319.8	74.2	3,649.4	91	2.5
Machinery and equipment	127.2	17.9	14	145.7	4.6	3.1	279.3	136.4	48.9	156.4	14.9	9.5
Electric machines and equipment	78.4	24.3	31	93.2	13.8	14.8	303	199.7	65.9	172.6	43.6	25.3
Radio, TV & communication equipment	215.1	121.8	56.6	196.1	14.3	7.3	609.8	491.4	80.6	310.2	250.2	80.6
Motor vehicles	77.1	48.7	63.2	51.7	22.8	44	405.9	357.3	88	148.4	108.5	73.1

Note: Exchange rates of VND 10,978 and VND12,938 per $1 have been used to convert data from VND to $ in 1994 and 1997. Outputs are at 1994 constant prices.
Source: GSO 1999b, 1999c.

United States and Korea have established a whole new industry with the capacity to assemble 83,260 vehicles annually, ranging from small family cars to large trucks (UNIDO and DSI 1999, pp. 165–9). Another example is in the electronics industry, where foreign investment has helped to produce the first made-in-Vietnam computer. The $25 million joint venture between the United States Harrison Industries and Vietnamese firms has produced a series of six models of computers, "Saigon 300", based on Harrison Industries' design. With an output of 2,000 units per month, the joint venture is estimated to take 10–20 percent of Vietnam's personal computer market that has previously been dominated by imported products from Taiwan and Singapore (Nguyen 1998; UNIDO and DSI 1999, p. 141).

FDI flows have also contributed to improving and extending of the existing production of import-substitution industries. In the iron and steel industry, three joint-ventures have been approved since the mid-1990s and those joint ventures have added 620,000 tons of capacity to existing capacity of 430,000 tons of local SOEs (Fukui 1998, p. 39).

The contribution of FDI flows to the development of infant import-substitution industries has also been reflected in the change of Vietnam's specialization ratio (SR)[4]. Overall, the specialization ratio of all industries that have been considered as infant import-substitution industries improved between 1991 and 1997, except in the cases of coke briquettes, oil products and nuclear fuel, and the metal and motor vehicle industries. In the case of the electric machinery and equipment industry, the specialization ratio was improved significantly from –0.93 in 1991 to –0.06 in 1997. In other words, the exports of Vietnam's electric machines and equipment were almost equal to its imports. As FDI flows have contributed significantly in increasing the capital stock as well as to the output of those industries, such improvements of the specialization ratio has been attributed substantially to FDI flows to Vietnam since 1988.

In conclusion, FDI flows have significantly promoted the development of infant import-substitution industries by creating whole new industries (such as the oil and gas, petrochemical, and automotive industries) or improving and extending existing ones. Between 1994 and 1998, FDI flows contributed to over 70 percent of the increase in capital of those infant supportive import-substitution industries and 14 percent of the increase in output of those industries. Such small contributions to increasing output may be attributed to the fact that many FIEs had just started their production and had not reached full operational capacity. However, the increase in FIEs output has contributed to the improvement of country's specialization ratio of infant import-substitution industries, and thus towards both a decrease in its dependence on imports and an increase in its ability to exports.

Impact of government policies

The positive and important contribution of FDI flows to the development of infant import-substitution industries in Vietnam since 1988 has been attributed to government policies that provide favourable and attractive conditions for foreign investors to invest in those industries. The government policies to attract FDI flows to those industries can be classified into four groups: domestic protection policies, tax incentives policies, the foreign currency balance, and local content requirement.

Domestic market protection for infant supportive import-substitution products has been the most important factor. Vietnam's domestic market protection includes high tariffs on imports and import licences and quotas on items also produced by infant supportive import-substitution industries. These tariffs are as high as 200 percent for motor vehicles. Moreover, the general exception and temporary exclusion lists of Vietnam's tariff reduction schedule under the ASEAN Free Trade Area (AFTA) programme have included a majority of products by infant import-substitution industries in order to protect them from competition for as long as it is allowed under AFTA. Those products are:

- all kinds of vehicles, including motorcycles;
- bicycles and toys;
- home appliances;
- cosmetics and non-essential products;
- all types of fabrics and several types of garments;
- all types of iron and steel; and
- general mechanical products.

These products accounted for over 41 percent of the items listed in reduction schedule in 1998 (MOF 1998, p. 31).

Besides tariff protection, the local market for import-substitution products has also been protected by import quotas and licences. In 1998, for instance, import quotas were set for petroleum, fertilizers, cement, construction glass, paper, sugar, and steel of various kinds. Imports of used consumer goods, used automobile spare parts, automobiles and motorcycles were also banned (IMF 1999, p. 61).

A second group of government incentives is tax incentives given to FDI projects to develop infant import-substitution industries. A profit tax of 15 percent applying for 10 years, two years' tax exemption, and three years' tax deduction of 50 percent from the time projects start making a profit is granted for FDI projects that invest in metallurgy, basic chemicals, mechanics, petrochemicals, fertilizer, electronic accessories, and automotive and motorcycle accessories (NPPH 1999).

94 *Foreign Direct Investment and Development in Vietnam*

The third group relates to government policies guaranteeing the foreign currency balance for FDI projects that produce import substitutions. While ordinary FDI projects have to balance the foreign currency needed by themselves, the government will sell foreign currency to meet the production demands of FDI projects that produce import substitutions belonging to the above industries.

The fourth group of policies relates to local content requirements. As mentioned in Chapter 3, local content requirements are specified in each project licence (where applicable, especially for the automotive and motorcycle industries). The purpose of local content requirements is to require foreign investors to establish the supportive industries to produce necessary accessories locally. In addition, a profit tax of 20 percent, tax exemption of one year, and tax deduction of 50 percent for two years from the time when projects start making profits will be given to projects that make products with high local content (NPPH 1999). While this achieved some initial results as mentioned in Chapter 3, the establishment of supportive industries, especially in the automotive and electronic industries, has faced several difficulties due to the lack of local capacity and low domestic demand for final products.

In short, the government policies designed to attract FDI flows to develop infant supportive import-substitution industries have had positive effects to different extents. This conclusion is supported by the regression analysis on factors that influenced the performance of FIEs in 1998. While the full details of the regression analysis appear in Appendix 2, the major result of the regression analysis is as follows:

$$\text{PROFIT} = 0.102 + 0.14 \text{ PROTECT}^* - 0.139 \text{ FOREIGN}^{**} + 0.238 \text{ YEAR}^{***}$$
$$(0.19) \quad (1.9) \quad (-2) \quad (3.3)$$

$$- 0.544 \text{ TAX}^{***} - 0.018 \text{ TECH} - 0.012 \text{ WAGE}$$
$$(-7.9) \quad (-0.26) \quad (-0.18)$$

$\bar{R}^2 = 0.358$ D-W = 2.0 $F_{(6,132)} = 13.8^{***}$ SE = 1.2   N = 139
***, ** and * indicates significant at the 1, 5 and 10 percent level respectively. The figures in brackets are t-statistics.
PROFIT: Profit ratio of profit over revenue
TAX: Ratio of profit and revenue tax over revenue
PROTECT: Domestic market protection policies
FOREIGN: Foreign share in legal capital
TECH: Technology transfer
WAGE: Average wage of local labour
YEAR: The time that the projects operate in Vietnam

Compared to the result of previous regression analysis, this result shows that while government tax incentives facilitated the export performance and profit-making of FIEs, the domestic market protection policies attracted FDI to import substitution industries but discouraged the export performance of FIEs. These contradictory effects will require the close attention of the government in future.

The regression analysis on FIEs' performance and profit ratio has proved that, at least for 1998, government policies, especially tax incentives and the protection of the domestic market, played an important role in the performance of FIEs. By supporting the FIEs, government policies have contributed to attracting FDI flows to promote the infant import-substitution industries of Vietnam.

Conclusion

This chapter has examined the contribution of FDI flows to the industrialization process in Vietnam through transferring technology and management skills, and through the government's dual industrialization strategy. In terms of technology transfers, FDI flows have brought newer and better technology to Vietnam. An examination of several indices showed that FIEs have been more capital-intensive, generating higher productivity compared to local firms. Several government policies have been designed to promote the technology transfer process. However, some accompanying problems such as transfer pricing have occurred during the technological transfer process, and require close government attention.

FDI flows have also promoted industrial growth and increased the share of the industrial sector in the total output. Though only half of FDI flows have been channelled toward export-oriented industries, such FDI has been the major force behind the rapid growth of Vietnam's exports by providing needed capital, modern technology and access to international markets.

About half of FDI flows in Vietnam have focused on promoting the development of infant supportive import-substitution industries and FDI flows have contributed significantly in terms of increasing the capital stock of those industries, creating whole new industries or expanding and modernizing the existing industries.

The significant contribution of FDI flows to the industrialization process in Vietnam has been attributed to the role of government policies such as tax policies and domestic protection policies. Regression analyses found that government tax incentives and protection policies have played a decisive role in the exports and performance of FIEs.

This chapter has shown that FDI flows may generate either positive or detrimental effects during the industrialization process, and this has really depended on government policies. In the case of Vietnam, the positive and significant contribution of FDI flows in the industrialization process, in promoting the development of both export-oriented industries as well as infant supportive import-substitution industries has been attributed to government policies of creating a favourable environment for the operation of FIEs, promoting the positive impacts and minimizing the detrimental effects of FDI flows.

Notes

A major part of Chapter 5 appeared in Pham, H.M. "The export performance of foreign invested enterprises in Vietnam". *ASEAN Economic Bulletin* 18, no. 3 (2001): 263–75.

[1] The value of machinery and equipment imported for FIEs is sometimes overvalued due to transfer pricing problems.

[2] Kojima's hypothesis divides FDI into two types: trade-oriented (the Japanese-type) and anti-trade-oriented (the American-type) based on comparative advantages and industrial structures. According to Kojima's theory, FDI flows to the industry in which a host country holds comparative advantage over the home country. This flow will promote an upgrading of industrial infrastructure on both sides and accelerate trade between the two countries. That is the case of Japanese FDI in Asian developing countries which focus on labour-intensive and resources-based industries, where host countries have a comparative advantage over Japan and hence create trade between Japan and Asian developing countries (Kojima 1978, 1991).

In contrast, American FDI is concentrated in capital-intensive and high technology industries and that pattern of American FDI has not made use of the host country's comparative advantage. Kojima argued that such investment of U.S. large and oligopolistic firms is anti-trade oriented and, in the long run, may lead to trade-substitution effects (Kojima 1978, 1991).

[3] Those industries are coke, oil products, chemical and chemical products, rubber and plastic products, non-metal products, metal, metal products, machinery and equipment, electric machinery and equipment, radios, televisions and communications equipment and motor vehicle industries.

[4] The specialization ratio has been calculated based on the following formula:

$$SR_{g,c} = (EXP_{g,c} - IMP_{g,c}) / (EXP_{g,c} + IMP_{g,c})$$

where:
- $SR_{g,c}$: Specialization ratio
- $EXP_{g,c}$: Exports of Vietnam
- $IMP_{g,c}$: Imports of Vietnam
- g : The product concerned
- c : trading partner, in this case is the whole world

The specialization ratio may change between –1 and +1 and when it is equal to +1, the host country specializes in producing the product concerned and when it is equal to –1, the host country has not produced sufficiently of the product concerned, and has imported them from overseas to meet domestic demand.

6
FDI, Vietnam's Regional Development and Poverty Alleviation

This chapter focuses on the impact of FDI on regional development and poverty alleviation. It will analyze the factors influencing the regional allocation of FDI flows and in turn, their impact on the growth of each region. This will be followed by an assessment of how FDI contributed to Vietnam's successful efforts to reduce poverty in the 1990s.

Overview of regional economic development

Vietnam is divided into seven geographic and socio-economic regions: the Red River Delta, Northern Uplands, North Central, Central Coast, Central Highlands, Southeast and the Mekong River Delta (See Figure 6.1).

As shown in Figure 6.1, the Northern Uplands is the largest region and accounts for 31.2 percent of the country's total land area. The Central Highlands and Central Coast are the next largest and account for 16.8 percent and 15.4 percent of the country's total land area respectively. The Red River Delta and Southeast regions are the smallest regions, accounting for 3.8 percent and 7.1 percent of the country's land area respectively.

However, the two smallest regions, in particular the Red River Delta, are also the most densely populated. While the Red River Delta and Southeast regions together made up less than 11 percent of the country's land area, they had over 36 percent of the country's population in 1999 (Table 6.1). By contrast, the Northern Uplands and Central Highlands, with 48 percent of the country's land area, are the least populated regions, accounting for only 21.1 percent of the country's population. The Red River Delta region including Ha Noi city, and the Southeast, including Ho Chi Minh City, are also the most developed regions in Vietnam. They are the major industrial centres,

Figure 6.1 Vietnam's Regions and Growth Triangles

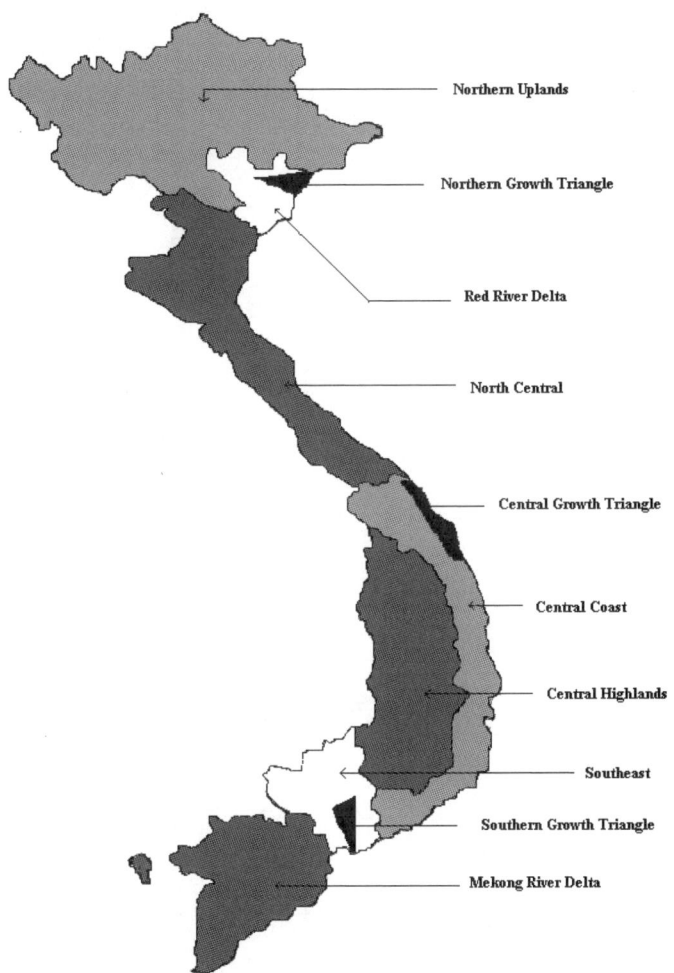

Source: Government of Vietnam and World Bank 1999, p. 15.

with 20.3 percent and 43 percent respectively of the country's industrial output in 1997. The Central Highlands, on the other hand, is the least industrialized region, with less than 1 percent of the national industrial output in 1997.

Table 6.1 Regions in Vietnam: General Indicators

Region	Industrial share 1997 (%)	Agriculture share 1997 (%)	Service share 1997 (%)	Population share 1999 (%)	Income per capita 1993 ($)	Income per capita 1997 ($)
Red River Delta	20.3	17.7	17.2	19.4	123.2	239.5
Northern Uplands	9.1	10.3	7.1	17.1	96.8	178.2
North Central	4.7	9.2	7.1	13.1	92.2	179.1
Central Coast	6.7	6.0	8.9	8.5	123.6	199.2
Central Highlands	0.9	5.4	2.1	4.0	108.1	195.9
Southeast	43.0	13.7	37.7	16.7	254.4	465.1
Mekong River Delta	15.2	37.8	20.1	21.1	141.6	219.0

Note: Income data are per capita income transferred into $ by using the exchange rates of VND 10,640 and VND 12,938 per $1 for 1993 and 1997 respectively.
Source: GSO 1996, 1999b, 1999c; GOV and World Bank 1999.

In terms of agricultural production, the Mekong River and Red River Deltas are the two major rice producing areas in Vietnam. The Southeast, Mekong River Delta and Red River Delta regions also house the most important service centres in Vietnam as the Vietnam's three largest cities—Ha Noi, Hai Phong and Ho Chi Minh City—are in those regions. Collectively, these regions also accounted for 75 percent of the total country's service output in 1997 (Table 6.1).

Clearly, the Southeast, Red River Delta and Mekong River Delta regions are the most developed regions in Vietnam, accounting for the largest share of industrial, agricultural, and service output. The living standards in those regions are accordingly the highest in Vietnam (Table 6.1). In particular, the annual per capita income of the Southeast (including Ho Chi Minh City) was more than twice that of other regions.

Recognizing the importance of regional development and the need to reduce inequality between regions, the government has created three economic growth triangles to boost development in the rest of the country. The growth triangles are Ha Noi-Hai Phong-Quang Ninh in the North, Quang Nam-Da Nang in the Centre and Ho Chi Minh City-Bien Hoa-Vung Tau in the south (Figure 6.1). With concentrated public investment to improve the infrastructure in the growth triangles, the government expects that they will attract large amount of domestic and foreign investment, achieve rapid growth and hence generate significant trickle-down effects to promote economic development in surrounding areas (Mundle and Arkadie 1997, p. 15).

Foreign direct investment flows and regional development

This section examines government policies and other factors affecting the regional allocation of FDI flows over the 1988–98 period and the effects of such investment on regional development.

Regional allocation of FDI and government policies

The uneven regional and provincial distribution of FDI between 1988 and 1998 reflected existing levels of development and geographical conditions. The more developed regions and provinces attracted significantly larger amounts of both committed and implemented FDI—the Southeast and Red River Delta regions alone accounted for 82.4 percent of total FDI commitment[1] (Table 6.2). This regional pattern is also reflected in the major cities, where Ha Noi, Hai Phong and Ho Chi Minh cities together accounted for 54.7 percent of committed FDI

Table 6.2 Provincial Allocation of Foreign Direct Investment in Vietnam, 1988–98 (percent)

		Committed FDI							Implemented FDI
	1988–98	1988–93	1994	1995	1996	1997	1998		1991–98
Total	**100.0**	**100.0**	**100.0**	**100.0**	**100.0**	**100.0**	**100.0**		**100.0**
Red River Delta	**30.0**	**30.5**	**35.6**	**22.8**	**37.7**	**26.3**	**12.6**		**32.8**
Ha Noi	22.2	22.1	24.8	15.3	29.9	17.4	11.8		22.3
Hai Phong	4.3	7.3	7.8	2.1	1.7	7.2	0.2		6.8
Ha Tay	1.4	0.5	2.4	1.0	2.7	0.5	0.3		1.8
Hai Hung	1.7	0.3	0.2	3.3	3.4	0.8	0.3		1.5
Three other provinces	0.4	0.2	0.5	1.0	0.1	0.5	0.0		0.3
Northern Uplands	**4.7**	**0.8**	**2.5**	**4.6**	**6.4**	**8.2**	**0.6**		**3.8**
Quang Ninh	2.5	0.2	1.5	0.5	4.2	6.3	0.0		0.8
Vinh Phu	1.2	0.2	0.5	2.0	2.0	1.4	0.0		1.9
Ha Bac	0.4	0.0	0.4	1.8	0.0	0.1	0.0		0.9
Ten other provinces	0.5	0.4	0.2	0.3	0.2	0.4	0.6		0.2
North Central	**2.5**	**0.9**	**3.2**	**5.2**	**1.0**	**3.4**	**0.4**		**3.4**
Thanh Hoa	1.2	0.1	1.7	5.2	0.0	0.0	0.0		1.9
Nghe An	0.6	0.1	0.0	0.0	0.9	2.7	0.0		0.3
Thua Thien-Hue	0.4	0.5	1.0	0.0	0.1	0.7	0.1		1.0
Three other provinces	0.2	0.2	0.4	0.0	0.0	0.0	0.3		0.2
Central Coast	**7.8**	**4.2**	**4.1**	**4.8**	**3.9**	**4.4**	**29.5**		**3.4**
Quang Nam-Da Nang	3.0	3.3	2.4	4.1	2.2	3.9	0.7		1.8
Quang Ngai	3.9	0.0	0.1	0.0	0.0	0.1	28.2		0.0
Three other provinces	1.0	0.9	1.5	0.7	1.7	0.4	0.5		1.6
Central Highlands	**0.2**	**0.1**	**0.1**	**0.2**	**0.0**	**0.6**	**0.2**		**0.3**
Kontum	0.0	0.0	0.0	0.0	0.0	0.0	0.0		0.0
Gia Lai	0.1	0.0	0.1	0.0	0.0	0.6	0.0		0.2
Dac Lac	0.1	0.1	0.0	0.2	0.0	0.0	0.2		0.2

(continued)

Table 6.2 Provincial Allocation of Foreign Direct Investment in Vietnam, 1988–98 (percent) (continued)

	Committed FDI							Implemented FDI
	1988–98	1988–93	1994	1995	1996	1997	1998	1991–98
Southeast	**52.4**	**57.1**	**42.1**	**58.3**	**47.1**	**51.9**	**38.2**	**50.6**
Ho Chi Minh City	28.2	41.6	23.9	28.4	24.4	23.2	14.8	26.8
Song Be	4.1	1.1	6.3	1.9	5.5	5.7	4.4	5.5
Tay Ninh	0.6	0.1	0.1	2.2	0.3	0.1	0.1	0.8
Dong Nai	9.9	9.7	9.0	17.5	6.1	10.8	2.5	13.8
Ba Ria-Vung Tau	6.7	3.6	2.3	7.6	10.6	10.2	0.4	2.8
Three other provinces	2.9	1.1	0.6	0.6	0.2	1.8	15.9	0.9
Mekong River Delta	**2.5**	**2.5**	**8.0**	**1.0**	**1.1**	**2.0**	**1.2**	**5.6**
Can Tho	0.4	0.4	0.8	0.2	0.0	1.1	0.3	0.3
Long An	0.7	0.5	1.2	0.6	0.5	0.7	0.8	1.4
Kien Giang	0.7	0.6	4.7	0.0	0.0	0.1	0.0	3.2
Eight other provinces	0.6	1.1	1.3	0.3	0.6	0.1	0.0	0.8

Note: The data do not include FDI flows to the oil and gas industries.
Source: GSO 1995; 1996a; 1997; 1998a; 1999a and several World Bank Country Reports.

flows. The other five regions received less than 20 percent of total committed FDI flows. The Central Highlands, for example, received merely 0.2 percent of total committed FDI. The Red River Delta and Southeast regions, especially Ha Noi, Hai Phong and Ho Chi Minh City, have accounted for 83.4 percent and 55.9 percent of total implemented FDI flows respectively. Ho Chi Minh City and four other surrounding provinces in the Southeast accounted for almost half of the total committed and implemented FDI flows in Vietnam over the 1988–98 period.

In terms of the sectoral allocation of FDI, the Southeast and the Red River Delta regions accounted for over 73 percent of committed and implemented FDI flows in the manufacturing sector, 89.1 percent of committed FDI flows and 96.4 percent of implemented FDI flows in the service sector, and over 50 percent of those in the primary sector.

The structure of FDI flows within each region also reflected each region's economic development level. Figure 6.2 shows that, except for the Central Highlands, FDI flows to the service sector have been relatively high in more developed regions. For the Red River Delta, Central Coast and Southeast regions (including the growth triangles), committed FDI flows into the service sector have been higher than those for the manufacturing and primary sectors (equal only to committed FDI flows in the manufacturing sector in the case of the Southeast).

Figure 6.2 Structure of Committed Foreign Direct Investment, 1988–98

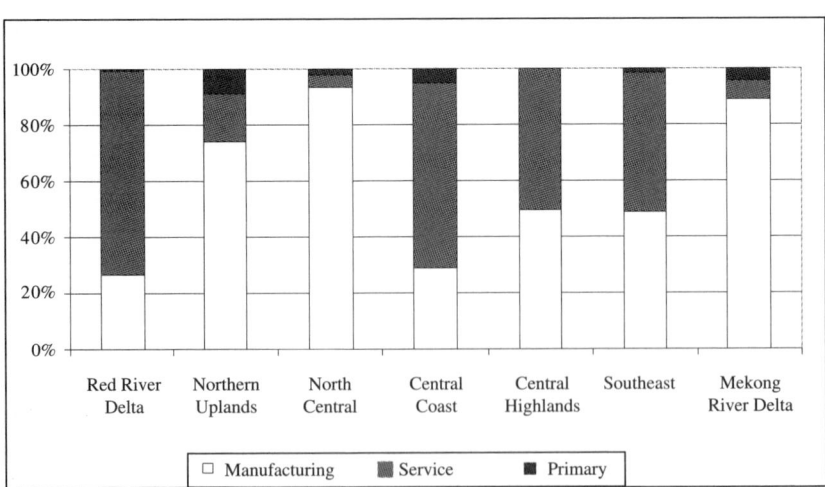

Note: The figure does not include FDI flows to the oil and gas industries.
Source: GSO 1995, 1996a; 1998a; 1999a and several World Bank Country Reports.

The large share of committed FDI in the service sector in three regions reflects the construction of hotel and office buildings, the increase in financial and banking services as well as other business and personal services. The high concentration of FDI in service sectors in these regions also shows the trend that the biggest cities such as Ha Noi, Ho Chi Minh City and Da Nang have become the country's key service centres.

The pattern has been for FDI flows to gradually diffuse from the most developed regions of Red River Delta and Southeast regions to less developed regions, and from a few large cities to surrounding provinces (Table 6.2). From 1988 to 1993, over 85 percent of committed FDI flows and over 90 percent of implemented FDI flows were concentrated in the Red River Delta and Southeast regions, especially in Ha Noi and Ho Chi Minh City. However, since 1994, FDI flows have gradually fanned out to other regions, especially the Northern Uplands and Central Coast regions. In 1998, these two regions accounted for over 30 percent of committed and 14.4 percent of implemented FDI flows. By contrast, Ha Noi, Hai Phong and Ho Chi Minh cities' combined share of committed FDI decreased from 71 percent between 1988 and 1993 to 26.8 percent in 1998. The jump in foreign investment in the Central Coast region in 1998, however, was due to the region hosting Vietnam's first oil refinery plant with total investment capital of $1.3 billion. FDI flows to other regions proceeded at a slower pace. The three other regions of North Central, Central Highlands and Mekong River Delta accounted for just 1.8 percent of committed FDI flows and 11.9 percent of implemented FDI flows in 1998.

The diffusion of foreign investment, especially from the Southeast toward the Northern part of the country, has been attributed to the following:

- increasing costs such as labour costs and property prices in the south;
- energy shortages in the south and surpluses in the north; and
- the improvement of infrastructure in the north (Gates and Truong 1994, pp. 16–19; Nestor 1997, pp. 188–9).

In terms of countries of origin, each group of foreign investors had its own regional focus. In general, the Southeast has been the most popular destination for investment from the Asian NICs, North America, Japan and the European Union. The Red River Delta region, on the other hand, has accounted for over 4.6 percent of FDI flows from Australia and New Zealand, and over 42.9 percent of FDI flows from the Association of Southeast Asian Nations (ASEAN). While only 21.1 percent of FDI from Asian NICs was to the Red River Delta region, about 32 percent of FDI from South Korea has been channelled to this region as South Korean investors shifted their focus toward Ha Noi and Hai Phong cities with the intention of getting closer to policy-making authorities (Nestor 1997, p. 192).

In short, FDI flows in Vietnam initially concentrated in the more developed Red River Delta and Southeast regions, especially the two biggest cities of Ha Noi and Ho Chi Minh City, and later showed some diffusion to the North and Central regions. The concentration of FDI flows in the two most developed regions also coincides with the government's economic growth triangle strategy.

To counterbalance the regional inequality of FDI flows, the Law on Foreign Direct Investment provided two sets of tax incentives in order to attract FDI to remote and mountainous areas or areas with difficult natural, economic and social conditions.

The first set relates to projects in mountainous or remote areas, which includes almost all provinces of the Northern Uplands, North Central and Central Coast regions, and all provinces of the Central Highlands and Mekong River Delta regions. A profit tax rate of 10 percent is given to FDI projects investing in establishing infrastructure in these areas (NPPH 1999). Infrastructure projects enjoy a profit tax exemption of four years and profit tax deductions of 50 percent for four years after the project starts making a profit. There is also an eight year profit tax exemption for infrastructure development and afforestation projects in mountainous or remote areas (NPPH 1999, pp. 47–50; pp. 289–93).

The second set of investment incentives relates to projects in areas not on the list of mountainous and remote areas, but having difficult natural, economic and social conditions; some of these lie within the more developed Red River Delta and Southeast regions (NPPH 1999, pp. 47–50; pp. 289–93). A profit tax rate of 15 percent is given to FDI projects located in these areas. In addition, these projects enjoy two years' exemption from profit tax and three years' profit tax deduction of 50 percent after the project starts making a profit.

Despite these government tax incentives, FDI did not rapidly flow to less developed regions and provinces. As of 1998, several of these provinces had recorded a very low or even zero share of committed and implemented FDI flows, especially in mountainous and remote areas. Quang Tri province in the Central Coast, Kon Tum province in the Central Highlands, and Bac Kan provinces in the Northern Uplands received no FDI project, while Ha Giang and Cao Bang provinces in Northern Uplands hosted only one FDI project each over the 1988–98 period. In terms of implemented FDI, the number of provinces without FDI flows increased to five. In general, FDI flows have remained concentrated in more developed regions and large cities where the infrastructure conditions is better. This conclusion is supported by the regression analysis below.

Factors influencing the provincial allocation of FDI

The concentration of FDI in more developed provinces and large cities is not unique to Vietnam but is also evident in several developing countries in Asia, Latin America and Eastern Europe. Several theories about the motivation for FDI flows have identified that a combination of market characteristics (such as regional market size or growth rates), government investment incentives (such as tax incentives), infrastructure, and the labour force influences the pattern of FDI distribution within countries.

The regression analysis below uses data on the regional allocation of FDI to identify factors that have influenced the regional distribution of such investment in Vietnam over the 1988–98 period. While the full details of the regression analysis appear in Appendix 3, the main results of regression analysis can be summarized as follows:

For committed FDI flows over the 1988–98 period:
LnFDI = 10.55 + 0.44 LnTEL*** + 0.23 LnINC* + 0.32 LnPUP*** + 0.16 LnTAX
       (1.53)   (3.4)   (1.74)   (3.2)   (1.4)

$\bar{R}^2$ = 0.517   D-W = 1.76 $F_{(4, 48)}$ = 14.9***   SE = 1.26   N = 53

For implemented FDI flows over the 1991–98 period:
LnFDI = 1.34 + 0.3 LnTEL** + 0.35 LnINC** + 0.25 LnPUP** + 0.23 LnTAX**
       (0.22)   (2.34)   (2.63)   (2.51)   (2.07)

$\bar{R}^2$ = 0.528   D-W = 1.88 $F_{(4, 48)}$ = 15.5***   SE = 1.1   N = 53

***, ** and * indicates significant at 1, 5 and 10 percent level respectively. The figures in brackets are the t-statistic.

FDI: provincial allocation of committed FDI flows for the 1988–98 period (or implemented FDI flows for the 1991–98 period).
TEL: average telephones per capita of each province
INC: income per capita of each province
PUP: number of middle secondary school pupil of each province
TAX: tax ratio of total FDI projects of each province

The regression analysis above finds that infrastructure, the quality of the labour force, and the size of the local market are the most important factors deciding the regional allocation of FDI flows. The government's tax incentives have not had a significant effect on attracting committed FDI flows as well as implementing committed FDI projects in mountainous or remote provinces. This result coincides with the fact that remote and mountainous provinces have received very small amounts of FDI flows compared to more developed provinces and cities, although the government has offered tax incentives for FDI projects in those provinces.

Impact of FDI on regional development

Although FDI flows have promoted overall regional economic development, this impact has been unevenly distributed between Vietnam's seven regions, with foreign investment concentrated in the largest cities, the Red River Delta, and the Southeast.

In the period under review, the impact of FDI on regional economic development was mainly in the industrial sector, which attracted the largest share of foreign investment; FDI in the service sector was present in only sixteen provinces, and only a small amount of FDI went to agriculture.

By 1998, the capital of foreign invested enterprises (FIEs) accounted for a major share of the total in several regions in Vietnam. In the Southeast, which received the largest share of FDI flows, the capital of FIEs accounted for 71.6 percent of the region's total industrial capital, almost four times that of SOEs and more than eight times that of private enterprises. While the Red River Delta region ranks second in terms of receiving FDI flows, FIE capital made up only 28 percent of the region's industrial capital and less than half of SOE capital as many SOEs are concentrated in the Red River Delta. Moreover, as shown in Figure 6.2, most FDI flows to the Red River Delta region were actually channelled toward services and hence reduced the contribution of FDI flows to that region's industrial capital.

In contrast, the relatively small amounts of FDI flows to other regions has contributed significantly to these regions' hitherto scarce industrial capital. As shown in Table 6.3, in the case of the Northern Uplands, which received only 3.9 percent of total FDI, FIEs were the largest in terms of industrial capital. Similarly, the small amount of FDI flows to the North Central and the Central Coast made up more than 30 percent of those regions' total industrial capital. Only in the case of the Central Highlands and Mekong River Delta did FIEs account for the smallest share of industrial capital.

Table 6.3 also shows that, in general, the contribution of FIEs in the regions' industrial turnover increased over the 1995–98 period. However, the unequal allocation of FDI flows between regions, and hence the unequal share of output generated by FIEs, led to the unequal contribution of FIEs to regional industrial output. As shown in Table 6.3, FIEs accounted for the largest share of industrial output in the Southeast while ranking second in the Red River Delta and Northern Uplands. In other regions, FIEs accounted for less than 10 percent of the industrial output.

In terms of contribution to regional industrial output growth, FIEs in the Red River Delta and the Southeast regions contributed to between half to two-thirds of regional industrial output growth over the

Table 6.3 Structure of Regional Industrial Output, 1995–98 (percent)

	Northern Uplands				Red River Delta				North Central				Central Coast				Central Highland				Southeast				Mekong River Delta			
	'95	'96	'97	'98	'95	'96	'97	'98	'95	'96	'97	'98	'95	'96	'97	'98	'95	'96	'97	'98	'95	'96	'97	'98	'95	'96	'97	'98
1. Output																												
SOEs	75.9	75.6	74.0	66.4	57.7	54.5	51.7	50.2	64.0	62.5	62.0	59.7	56.3	58.3	58.3	57.6	33.4	32.4	30.2	28.5	38.8	37.4	35.7	33.5	45.7	48.0	48.6	50.1
Private sector	18.0	16.9	15.7	13.9	25.5	25.3	24.2	23.6	32.1	32.9	31.9	31.0	35.2	34.4	33.1	33.1	64.8	65.3	66.8	67.1	20.5	20.3	19.6	18.8	46.6	45.7	44.9	42.4
FIEs	6.0	7.5	10.3	19.7	16.7	20.2	24.0	26.3	3.9	4.6	6.1	9.3	8.5	7.3	8.6	9.3	1.9	2.3	3.0	4.4	40.7	42.3	44.7	47.7	7.7	6.4	6.5	7.5
2. Output Growth Rate																												
Total		13.6	14.9	17.9		13.3	18.2	12.0		7.6	10.4	8.9		12.3	16.1	11.1		12.5	10.4	7.6		16.4	13.3	12.3		7.5	8.7	8.5
Contribution of FIEs*		2.4	4.4	12.9		6.2	8.2	5.4		1.1	2.1	4.0		–0.3	2.7	1.8		0.7	1.0	1.5		8.6	8.3	8.9		–0.9	0.7	1.6

*Region's FIEs contribution in year t = $\dfrac{\text{(Region's FIEs output in year t – Region's FIEs output in year t-1)}}{\text{Region's output in year t-1}}$

Source: GSO 1998, 1999c.

1995–98 period. Elsewhere, such FIE contributions remained low except in the Northern Uplands in 1998 (Table 6.3).

In conclusion, the analysis here shows that provinces or cities with better infrastructure, a more skilled labour force, and larger local markets have attracted more FDI. Thus, although foreign direct investment has contributed significantly to development at the provincial and regional levels by increasing capital stock and output, its impact has varied, reflecting the unequal allocation of FDI.

FDI and poverty alleviation

One important objective of the socio-economic development process in Vietnam is to tackle poverty. Foreign invested enterprises may contribute to poverty alleviation indirectly by promoting economic growth, or directly by generating employment and increasing income by paying higher wages and salaries. This section examines the poverty alleviation process in Vietnam and then analyzes the contribution of FDI.

Poverty alleviation

The results of two living standards surveys in 1993 and 1998 jointly conducted by the government of Vietnam and donors, including the World Bank, United Nations Development Program (UNDP) and Sweden's International Development Agency (SIDA), showed a "striking reduction in the incidence of poverty in Vietnam" (GOV and World Bank 1999, p. 4). The proportion of people classified as poor[2] declined from 58 percent in 1993 to 37 percent in 1998 while the figure for food poverty reduced from 25 percent in 1993 to 15 percent in 1998. This decrease of general poverty and food poverty in Vietnam within the short span of five years has been considered "very impressive" and "...no other country has recorded such a sharp decline in poverty in such a short period of time" (GOV and World Bank 1999, p. 4). In addition, social indicators including primary and secondary school enrolment, child and adult nutrition, access to infrastructure, and ownership of consumer durables improved between 1993 and 1998 (Table 6.4).

The agriculture, manufacturing and sales sectors recorded the highest reduction in poverty incidence. The achievement in the agricultural sector is especially significant as both living standard surveys, in 1993 and 1998, found that 90 percent of the poor (nearly 80 percent of whom depended on agriculture for their livelihoods), lived in rural Vietnam. However, while the incidence of poverty was reduced significantly between 1993 and 1998, income inequality

Table 6.4 Social Indicators of Vietnam, 1993–98 (percent)

		1993	1998
Human development			
Education			
Primary enrolment rate (net):	Female	87.1	90.7
	Male	86.3	92.1
Lower secondary enrolment rate (net):	Female	29.0	62.1
	Male	31.2	61.3
Upper enrolment rate (net):	Female	6.1	27.4
	Male	8.4	30.0
Child nutrition			
Incidence of stunting among children 0–59 months		51.0	34.0
Adult nutrition			
Incidence of moderate and severe malnutrition in adults		32.0	28.0
Access to infrastructure			
% of rural population with public health centre within the commune		93.0	97.0
Ownership rates of consumer durable			
% of households owing a television		25.0	58.0

Source: Modified from Table 1.2 in GOV and World Bank 1999, p. 7.

in Vietnam (measured by the Gini coefficient) increased slightly, from 0.33 in 1993 to 0.35 in 1998. Despite this, Vietnam is still a moderately equal society as its Gini coefficient is similar to those of South Asian countries (i.e. Bangladesh, India) and lower than those of Indonesia or Thailand (GOV and World Bank 1999, p. 70).

Regionally, there were divergences in poverty alleviation (Table 6.5). The Red River Delta, North Central and Southeast regions achieved the highest reduction of poverty incidence, while the Mekong River Delta, Central Coast, and Central Highlands recorded the lowest. In terms of real per capita expenditure, Table 6.5 shows that between 1993 and 1998, the Red River Delta, Southeast and North Central Coast regions also achieved the highest increase of real per capita expenditure, while the Mekong Delta, the Central Highlands and the Central Coast are the regions with the lowest increase of real per capita expenditure.

Thus, while Vietnam on the whole achieved significant reductions in the incidence of poverty, this has been distributed unevenly between the regions, with the more developed regions enjoying a larger reduction of poverty incidence over the 1993–98 period.

112 *Foreign Direct Investment and Development in Vietnam*

Table 6.5 Regional Poverty Situation in Vietnam, 1993 and 1998 (percent)

	Incidence of poverty of region		Contribution to poverty by region		Growth in real per capital expenditure
	1993	1998	1993	1998	1993–98
Red River Delta	79.0	59.0	21.0	28.0	31.0
Northern Uplands	63.0	29.0	23.0	15.0	55.0
North Central	75.0	48.0	16.0	18.0	46.0
Central Coast	50.0	35.0	10.0	10.0	29.0
Central Highlands	70.0	52.0	4.0	5.0	25.0
Southeast	33.0	8.0	7.0	3.0	78.0
Mekong River Delta	47.0	37.0	18.0	21.0	18.0

Source: Compiled based on data in Table 1.5, Figures 4.1; 4.2 and 4.3 in GOV and World Bank 1999, pp. 15–17 and pp. 71–72.

Impact of FDI

This section examines the contribution of FDI flows to poverty alleviation by assessing the amount of employment that has been created by FDI flows during the 1988–98 period. While Vietnam's large and growing labour force is one of the country's comparative advantages, population growth demands that the government create enough new jobs to absorb annual increases. As unemployment or underemployment is a principle reason for poverty, generating employment will contribute to the poverty alleviation process.

As mentioned in Chapter 3, Vietnam's labour force has increased at an annual growth rate of 3.5 percent, and every year, 1.2 million people have entered the labour market. Thanks to the government's reforms, millions of new job places have been created and an annual real employment growth rate of 1.8 percent was achieved during the 1993–98 period. The service and industry sectors remain the largest job providers, accounting for over 80 percent of total newly created employment. Unemployment and under-employment rates in Vietnam actually decreased from 3.7 percent and 66 percent in 1993 to 2.2 percent and 57 percent in 1998. However, these gains were threatened by the regional financial crisis that slowed down the growth rate of the whole economy in 1997 (World Bank 1998, p. 11).

Foreign investment flows since 1988 have contributed to the employment generation process in Vietnam by providing much needed investment capital, training, and modern technology. While public and domestic private savings and investment have been limited, FDI flows have played an important role in generating new employment—as creating one job place in a small or medium enterprise needs $800, while in SOEs this requires about $18,000 (World Bank 1998, p. 29). By the end of 1998, FDI flows had directly generated 270,000 job places, accounting for under 1 percent of Vietnam's total labour force, and indirectly created thousands of other jobs. It has been estimated that total employment directly and indirectly created by FDI flows was between 350,000 to 400,000.

The data on employment in FDI projects classified by regions and by sector for the whole 1988–1998 period, however, are not available. Table 6.6 shows the employment data in FDI projects for the 1994–96 period. As the greater part of FDI flows is concentrated in the Red River Delta and Southeast regions, it is not surprising that these regions also account for over 85 percent of the total employment generated by FDI. The Southeast region alone accounted for over 70 percent of total employment during the 1994–96 period. Table 6.6 shows that joint venture and 100 percent foreign-owned FDI projects are the most important in terms of employment generation. As the 100 percent foreign-owned projects increasingly became an important form of FDI, the amount of employment generated by these enterprises has also increased, from 29.1 percent in 1994 to 47.1 percent in 1996.

Manufacturing is the dominant sector in terms of employment generation, accounting for over 75 percent of employment generated by FDI flows during the 1994–96 period. On the other hand, the service sector accounted for just over 10 percent of total employment and agriculture, forestry and fishery accounted for just over 3 percent of total employment generation.

However, it has been very costly to generate each job place within FDI projects. Table 6.6 shows that mining is the most expensive sector in terms of capital investment needed to employ one person. Electricity, gas and water supply projects ranked second and other service activities (including banking and finance services) ranked third in terms of capital investment needed to create each job place. Employment generation in the agricultural, forestry, fishery, and manufacturing sectors have been the cheapest, as those sectors are labour intensive and require less capital to create each job place. It is generally more expensive to create one job place within an FDI project compared with either the local private sector or SOEs.

The 1998 industrial sector survey provided more details about employment in FIEs. In general, the job creation effects of FDI flows in the industrial sector have been insignificant. Industrial employment in FDI projects increased from 6.8 percent of total industrial employment in 1995 to 9.1 percent in 1998. Except in the case of the Southeast region, the share of FDI-generated employment in the total industrial

Table 6.6 Labour Working in Foreign Invested Projects, 1994–96

	31/12/1994		31/12/95		30/06/96		Capital per job 1996 ($)
	Labour (person)	Share in total (%)	Labour (person)	Share in total (%)	Labour (person)	Share in total (%)	
1. By regions	**88,054**	**100.0**	**139,678**	**100.0**	**172,925**	**100.0**	n.a.
Red River Delta	11,387	12.9	19,751	14.1	21,704	12.6	92,518
Northern Uplands	2,725	3.1	3,290	2.4	4,348	2.5	31,877
North Central	626	0.7	1,231	0.9	1,260	0.7	100,794
Central Coast	4,295	4.9	7,286	5.2	8,391	4.9	26,528
Central Highland	1,239	1.4	2,783	2.0	2,898	1.7	28,433
Southeast	63,578	72.2	99,597	71.3	128,197	74.1	53,308
Mekong River Delta	4,204	4.8	5,740	4.1	6,127	3.5	46,581
2. By forms of FDI	**88,054**	**100.0**	**139,678**	**100.0**	**172,925**	**100.0**	n.a.
100 % foreign owned	25,649	29.1	56,115	40.2	81,497	47.1	n.a.
Joint venture	60,327	68.5	81,121	58.1	88,658	51.3	n.a.
Business co-operation contract	2,078	2.4	2,442	1.7	2,770	1.6	n.a.
3. By sectors	**88,054**	**100.0**	**139,678**	**100.0**	**172,925**	**100.0**	n.a.
Agriculture & forestry	1,621	1.9	3,134	2.2	3,422	2.0	14,991
Fishery	1,140	1.3	1,246	0.9	1,196	0.7	17,642
Mining	5,517	6.3	5,712	4.1	6,202	3.6	550,000
Manufacturing	66,474	75.5	108,918	78.0	139,621	80.7	24,541
Electricity, gas & water supply	72	0.1	192	0.1	297	0.2	391,582
Construction	846	1	2,011	1.4	2,558	1.5	76,466
Trade	343	0.4	508	0.4	726	0.4	51,240

(*continued*)

Table 6.6 Labour Working in Foreign Invested Projects, 1994–96 (continued)

	31/12/1994		31/12/95		30/06/96		Capital per job 1996 ($)
	Labour (person)	Share in total (%)	Labour (person)	Share in total (%)	Labour (person)	Share in total (%)	
Hotel & restaurant	5,673	6.4	8,227	5.9	8,212	4.7	117,328
Transport & communication	3,605	4.1	5,071	3.6	5,608	3.2	78,531
Others	2,727	3.1	4,659	3.3	5,083	2.9	203,561

Vietnam's labour force was 34.6 million and 35.8 million in 1995 and 1996 respectively.
Source: GSO 1996, 1998.

employment has been small and was less than 10 percent in 1998. In the North Central region, industrial employment in FDI projects accounted for only 0.7 percent of the region's total industrial labour force.

FDI also accounted for a large share of employment in sub-sectors such as the oil and gas, office machines, computer and calculator, and leather goods industries. Water, gas, and electricity generation and supply as well as mining are the most costly sub-industries, requiring around $300,000 to employ one local worker. The cheapest industries are the garments, leather goods and furniture industries which require between $4,800 to $6,000 to create one job place. Though the capital investment needed to create one job place in FDI projects generally decreased between 1996 and 1998, it has been many times higher than that of either state-owned or private enterprises. In the case of the mineral industry, it is about over 60 times higher than SOEs and over 1,400 times higher than private enterprises. Such high capital investment needed to employ one local worker reflects the capital-intensive nature of FDI projects in Vietnam.

However, export-oriented FIEs require less capital investment to create one job place in comparison with FIEs focusing on the local market. Among 452 FIEs in manufacturing and primary industries (excluding the oil and gas industries) in 1998, the FIEs that exported more than 50 percent of their 1998 revenue required $10,227 to create one job place while FIEs that exported less than 50 percent of their 1998 revenue needed $74,585 to create one job place[3].

While FDI flows have actually created a number of jobs, especially in the manufacturing sector, such employment generation effects were constrained by the Asian regional economic crisis and shortage of qualified local workers. The regional financial crisis and the slowdown of economic growth in neighbouring countries led to the reduction of demand for Vietnam's exports, including those produced by FIEs. It has been estimated that 8 to 10 percent of total employees or between 20,000 to 25,000 workers in FIEs such as garments, footwear and automobiles were made redundant as a consequence of the regional financial crisis.

Another reason that may limit the employment generation effects of FDI is the shortage of qualified local workers. Table 6.7 reveals that qualified workers accounted for a large share of the total labour force employed by FDI projects in 1995. The share of workers with a tertiary degree or above in the total labour force employed by FDI projects is higher than that of SOEs and private enterprises. The share of qualified technicians (including technicians and workers with a college qualification) in the total labour force employed by FDI projects has also been higher than those of private enterprises. This reflects the fact that modern technology transferred through FDI flows and the capital intensive nature of such projects require large numbers of qualified local workers.

Table 6.7 Labour Force Classified by Qualification, 1995

	Tertiary level or above	College level	Technician
State-owned enterprises	10.2	10.7	26.2
Private enterprises	6.0	4.2	8.3
FDI projects	13.5	5.7	11.2

Source: GSO 1998, p. 353.

The number of qualified local workers, however, has been low and insufficient to meet the requirements of FDI projects. The survey conducted in 1998 revealed that around 80 percent of the FIEs which responded complained that local labour did not have competent technical qualifications, knowledge of English or requisite discipline and they needed to be retrained (UNIDO 1999).

In short, while FDI flows in Vietnam have created thousands of jobs, the numbers are insignificant compared to the local labour force as a whole. Moreover, such effects were constrained by the Asian regional economic crisis and the shortage of skilled labour.

Salaries and wages in FDI projects

Besides creating jobs, FDI flows also contributed to poverty alleviation by paying higher salaries and wages. In general, the average wage of an employee working in an FIE was about 30 to 50 percent higher than that of one working in a local enterprise. Table 6.8 shows that the average wage of local labour working in FDI projects increased from $84 per month in 1994 and 1995 to $94 in 1996. The Southeast and Red River Delta regions again recorded the highest average wages, while regions with lower FDI recorded low average wages. However, the latter also recorded higher rates of average wage *increases* compared to other regions. Wage increases in the North Central region increased by almost 2.7 times between 1994 and 1996.

Business co-operation contract enterprises offered the highest average wages followed by joint ventures, while 100 percent foreign-owned firms offered the lowest average wages. The average wages of the agriculture, forestry and fishery as well as manufacturing sectors were the lowest, as those sectors are labour-intensive and require less highly qualified labour than other capital and modern technology-intensive sectors such mining, banking and finance. In the first six months of 1996, for example, the average wage of local workers in the mining sector was about ten times higher than that in the agriculture, fishery, forestry and manufacturing sectors. Average local wages, however, are still many times lower than those of foreign

118 *Foreign Direct Investment and Development in Vietnam*

Table 6.8 Monthly Income of Labour Working in Foreign Invested Projects

	Vietnam labour ($)			Foreign labour ($)		
	1994	1995	First 6 months 1996	1994	1995	First 6 months 1996
1. By regions						
Red River Delta	62	76	99	740	1,047	1,256
Northern Uplands	37	52	71	263	555	1,157
North Central	33	75	89	438	626	796
Central Coast	39	48	53	391	644	977
Central Highland	43	38	54	306	565	707
Southeast	96	92	99	1,355	1,365	1,671
Mekong River Delta	56	68	78	1,063	714	667
2. By forms of FDI						
100% foreign-owned	40	41	52	643	764	993
Joint venture	101	111	131	885	1,050	1,367
Business co-operation contract	134	163	155	6,630	6,252	6,557

Source: GSO 1998.

labour, which increased from $1,164 in 1994 to $1,518 in 1996 (GSO 1998).

In short, FDI flows have contributed to the poverty alleviation process in Vietnam by increasing the income of labour working in FDI projects. However, the general impact of FDI flows on poverty alleviation in Vietnam, especially on employment generation, have depended very much on government policies.

Government policy

The general government policy has been to encourage foreign investors to employ local labour. Where sufficiently well qualified local labour cannot be found and foreign workers are employed, foreign investors are encouraged to train locals to replace foreign employees. The government has issued several regulations to protect the rights of local workers such as the right to strike and the rights of female workers (NPPH 1999). In particular, the government has determined a minimum wage as the basis for labour contract negotiations[4]. Despite a number of regulations to protect local workers and at the same time promote FDI flows to make use of the cheap local labour force, there are still disputes over wages and working conditions. In 1998, for example, there were 30 labour disputes and strikes related to FDI projects (VIR 1999).

Thus, although FDI flows in Vietnam since 1988 have contributed to the success of Vietnam in alleviating poverty incidence from 58 percent in 1993 to 37 percent in 1998 by creating employment opportunities and paying higher wages, the impact has not been significant for several reasons.

First, FDI flows have not created a significant number of jobs. As mentioned earlier, employment created by FDI accounted for less than 1 percent of the Vietnam's total labour force which stood at around 37 million in 1997 (GSO 1999, p. 10). In the industrial sector, which received the major share of FDI, the percentage of the labour force working in FIEs was less than 10 percent of the total industrial workforce (GSO 1999c). In contrast, local private enterprises accounted for 64.3 percent and SOEs accounted for 24.2 percent (GOV and World Bank 1999, p. 61). Compared to Vietnam's National Programme for job promotion,[5] which started in 1996, the employment opportunities created by FDI flows has been insignificant.

Second, the low effectiveness of FDI in terms of employment generation is partly attributable to the fact that a large proportion of FDI flows in Vietnam has been channelled to import substitution industries. Creating one job place in import substitution industries requires in excess of seven times the capital investment required in export-oriented industries. If all FDI flows over the 1988–98 period had been channelled to export-oriented industries, the number of job places created by FDI flows would have been many times higher.

Third, although employees working in FDI projects have been paid higher wages, this has not contributed significantly to the poverty alleviation process. Almost 100 percent of FDI flows focused on the industrial and service sectors, but 90 percent of poor people live in rural areas and nearly 80 percent of poor people work mainly in the agricultural sector. FDI flows thus had little direct impact on improving the living standards of the majority of the poor. The 1998 living standards survey revealed that in the rural areas, the improvement in living standards was attributed mainly to rising agricultural income and the diversification of agricultural incomes from farm and off-farm activities (GOV and World Bank 1999, p. 51).

Fourth, FDI flows may have also contributed also to widening the gap in living standards between the regions due to their unequal contribution to regional economic growth. The 1998 living standards survey found that the increase in inequality between regions explained 83 percent of the increase in total income inequality in Vietnam between 1993 and 1998, while the increase in inequality within regions accounted for only 17 percent of the increase in total income inequality (GOV and World Bank 1999, pp. 71–3).

Finally, rather than the FDI, the success of poverty alleviation in Vietnam has been attributed to the wider strategy of liberalization:

> The *doi moi* policies initiated in the late 1980's have led to rapid growth in GDP....The opportunities for employment and income generation that such rapid growth has created explain much of Vietnam's achievements in poverty alleviation.
>
> (GOV and WB 1999, p.41).

Hence FDI has only indirectly contributed to poverty alleviation in Vietnam by promoting rapid economic growth to the economy on a whole.

Conclusion

In general, FDI flows in Vietnam during the 1988–98 period were:
- unequally distributed between regions and provinces; and
- heavily concentrated in the Red River Delta and Southeast, especially in large cities such as Ha Noi, Hai Phong and Ho Chi Minh City.

This situation improved more recently as FDI flows started to diffuse to other surrounding regions and provinces.

The regression analysis on the factors influencing the provincial allocation of FDI flows found that the level of infrastructure, the quality of the labour force and the local market played a decisive role in attracting FDI. Regions and provinces with better infrastructure, a more highly qualified labour force and larger local market received correspondingly larger amounts of FDI. Government policies, especially tax incentives to promote the diffusion of FDI flows to mountainous and remote provinces, have not played as decisive a role as the development of regional infrastructure. While FDI flows have contributed positively to local development by increasing the industrial capital stock and output, such contributions may have widened the gap between richer and poorer provinces.

Foreign Direct Investment in Vietnam has had no significant impact on the alleviation of poverty. While Vietnam has achieved a very impressive overall reduction of poverty incidence, the contribution of FDI flows to this process through employment generation has been marginal. The capital-intensive nature of several FDI projects in import substitution industries, the regional financial crisis and the shortage of qualified local workers are other reasons that have prevented foreign investors from employing more local workers. Moreover, the heavy concentration of FDI in the industrial and service sectors has further limited the role of FDI flows as over 80 percent of the poor live and work in the rural agricultural sector. Furthermore, the unequal allocation of FDI between regions contributed to the increase in regional inequality in Vietnam. The contribution of FDI to poverty alleviation in Vietnam has been, therefore, indirect, through promoting rapid economic growth that, in turn, creates greater employment opportunities and income for the poor.

Notes

[1] The data on regional allocation of FDI over the 1988–98 period do not include FDI flows to the oil and gas industry.

[2] The poverty line in Vietnam has been defined on the basis of per capita expenditure that covers the nutritional needs to provide 2100 calories per day and basic non-food needs. In monetary terms, the poverty line in Vietnam was VND 1.2 million ($83) in 1993 and VND 1.8 million ($128) in 1998 of per capita expenditure annually. Of the 1998 poverty line, VND 1.287 (or $92) has been set for expenditure on essential food (GOV and World Bank 1999, pp. 5–6).

[3] A 50 percent mark was chosen because FIEs which export over 50 percent of their revenue will enjoy government tax incentives.

[4] The monthly minimum wage rates for unskilled labour working in FDI projects in the large cities of Ha Noi and Ho Chi Minh City is $45; $40 for other medium cities and $35 elsewhere (NHHP 1999, pp. 1383–4).

[5] Vietnam's National Programme for job promotion intends to create employment for 6.5 million workers.

7
Policy Implications

This chapter suggests several important implications for policy drawn from the evidence of the impact of FDI on Vietnam between 1988 and 1998. These policy implications are significant because FDI flows to Vietnam began to decline after 1997 as a consequence of the regional economic crisis.

FDI as an important supplementary source of investment

The first policy implication is the recognition of FDI flows as an important supplementary source of investment.

While long-term economic development in Vietnam has to rely on local savings and investment, the analyses in previous chapters show that FDI flows have contributed significantly to gross investment and economic growth. In general, FDI flows have directly contributed to around one-third of gross investment during the 1994–98 period and between 1 percent to 1.5 percent of annual GDP growth. In addition, FDI flows also indirectly contributed to socio-economic development by generating foreign exchange earnings, contributing to government budgets, and bringing in modern technology. On the other hand, the negative impact of FDI has been kept under control thanks to appropriate government policies. Several analyses have shown the need for co-operation between foreign investors, state-owned enterprises, and the private sector.

While FDI flows had an important impact on socio-economic development in Vietnam over the 1988–98 period, they have actually declined since the start of the Asian regional economic crisis in 1997. In the current economic climate, the government of Vietnam needs to improve the legal and operational environment and remove obstacles to the operation of foreign investment projects in order to attract more FDI flows.

First, the government needs to have a long-term strategy on foreign direct investment utilization. This will provide clear guidelines to foreign investors about government priorities given to FDI in the short, medium and long term. The lack of a clear strategy on FDI may have generated unnecessary confusion for foreign investors determining their long-term plans for doing business in Vietnam. That may also be the reason why a considerable number of foreign investors have invested in Vietnam for short-term benefits and immediately after, withdrawn their investment when the situation became less favourable.

Second, the government needs to improve the legal environment in order to attract more FDI flows. The regular review, and amendment when necessary, of laws and regulations regarding the operation of FDI projects will significantly improve Vietnam's attractiveness to foreign investors compared to other countries in the region. Since the regional crisis, several neighbouring countries have made significant policy changes (such as deregulating their economies and devaluing national currencies) in order to make their economies more attractive to foreign investors. Only regular reviews of relevant laws and regulations, especially those relating to wages, exports, tax incentives and foreign exchange management, will help Vietnam keep pace with its neighbours.

Third, bureaucratic efficiency needs to improve. Many changes in laws and regulations regarding FDI have not been implemented effectively due to bureaucratic inefficiency. The streamlining and improvement of the bureaucracy would include making laws and regulations more transparent; reducing the numbers of government agencies involved in the management and the operation of FDI projects; and decentralizing the management of FDI.

Fourth, improving the macroeconomic environment is another measure to attract more FDI flows. A high and stable economic growth rate, controllable inflation and appropriate exchange rate will increase foreign investor confidence in Vietnam and create more business opportunities to attract FDI flows.

Fifth, government policies that helped to maximize the positive impacts and minimize the detrimental effects of FDI so far should be maintained. These include the insistence on local content, local resource development, local partners (for some sectors), exports, and minimum wage requirements. While those requirements have been eased recently in accordance with the development of the local economy and the changes in the international market, they are still needed. However, the extent and the ways to implement those requirements should be adjusted in accordance with existing socio-economic conditions in Vietnam.

With FDI being an important supplementary source of investment, several changes and improvements in government policy are required to attract more FDI flows to Vietnam in the future.

Channelling FDI into export-oriented industries

The second policy implication is to attract more FDI flows into export-oriented industries that will make use of Vietnam's comparative advantages of cheap but relatively well educated labour.

As mentioned in chapter 5, only 36.2 percent of committed and 51 percent of implemented FDI flows in the primary and manufacturing sectors have actually been channelled to the industries in which Vietnam has high comparative advantages, while the rest has been focused on capital-intensive industries. As analyzed in chapters 4, 5, and 6, this is the reason why FDI flows have had an insignificant impact in generating employment and yet achieved low efficiency of performance. The significant movement of FDI flows toward export-oriented industries to exploit Vietnam's comparative advantage of cheap labour will, therefore, generate more employment, improve the efficiency of FDI projects and hence contribute substantially to the poverty alleviation process.

On the other hand, there is huge potential for FDI flows into export-oriented industries. A cross-country study by Wood and Mayer (1998) using 1990 data from 115 countries found that, the higher the proportion of skilled workers relative to land, the higher the share of manufacturing exports relative to primary exports (Wood and Mayer 1998 in GOV and World Bank 1999, p. 166). Based on this result, Belser (1999) has estimated that in 1997, for example, the manufacturing exports of Vietnam would have been 63 percent of total exports (or $9.88 billion) instead of actual figure of 37 percent (or $3.37 billion) (Belser 1999 in GOV and World Bank 1999, p. 166). The potential of a $6.5 billion increase in manufacturing exports shows the huge potential for the development of export-oriented industries in Vietnam.

An examination of 535 FDI projects in the industries in which Vietnam possesses comparative advantage (such as food processing, textiles, garments, leather products, wooden furniture, and electronics) shows that in 1998, those projects generated exports of $1.25 billion compared to the total investment of $2.5 billion. In other words, $1 of FDI in those industries generated $0.5 of exports. Hence, if this ratio holds for the future, $13 billion of FDI flows will be needed to achieve the $6.5 billion increase in manufacturing exports. However, the promotion of FDI flows into export-oriented industries requires several necessary measures.

First, the government needs to establish a long-term plan to develop export-oriented industries. This may initially focus on developing downstream, simple assembly and labour-intensive industries and later more technologically sophisticated, capital-intensive industries that produce middle and upstream products.

Second, tax preferences to FDI projects in export-oriented industries should be provided. The regression analysis in chapter 5 found that tax incentives played a decisive role in the export performance of FIEs in the sense that the lower the tax rates, the higher the export ratio. The regular review of tax preferences for FDI projects in export-oriented industries will guarantee that the tax incentives provided by the government of Vietnam will not be less favourable than those of other countries in the region.

Third, providing other forms of support for FDI projects in export-oriented industries will be beneficial. Such support may range from deregulating export and import activities; providing necessary information on the international market; improving infrastructure such as roads, ports, and airports; and developing supporting industries. The aim should be to create more favourable conditions for FDI projects investing in export-oriented industries.

Finally, gradually reducing domestic market protection is desirable. The result of the regression analysis in chapter 5 shows that domestic protection negatively correlated with export performance of FDI projects as foreign investors found that producing for the protected domestic market was easier than for the competitive international market. During the 1988–98 period, Vietnam's local market was protected by several tariff and non-tariff barriers. However, the reduction of domestic market protection requires careful consideration.

Reduction of protection

The third policy implication is the need to determine a plan to gradually reduce the protection for local markets and infant industries, although infant supportive capital-intensive industries still play an important role in the industrialization process in Vietnam. This would include the limiting of protection to a few key industries and applying protection measures in conformity with the requirements of international trade organizations such as the World Trade Organization (WTO).

As mentioned in Chapter 5, 63.8 percent of committed FDI flows and 49 percent of implemented FDI flows in the primary and manufacturing sectors have been channelled to capital-intensive industries. The concentration of FDI in capital-intensive industries has been attributed to the government's dual industrialization policy and intensive domestic protection. FDI flows have contributed to the establishment of several new industries or the modernization of the existing ones (such as the oil and gas, automobile and telecommunications industries). However, the low efficiency of many FIEs, the need to concentrate FDI flows in export-oriented industries, and the economic integration process in Vietnam require the limitation of protection to a few key industries.

Such reductions should not be carried out too quickly. The result of regression analysis in chapter 5 shows that protection played a decisive role in FIEs' performance and hence any immediate removal of protection will be unnecessarily detrimental to Vietnam's industrialization.

Moreover, the socio-economic conditions of Vietnam still require the development of some key infant supportive industries. The development strategy of Vietnam should not be based solely on low cost labour and abundant but finite natural resources. The experience of several countries shows that to avoid the low cost labour trap and to create sustainable development, Vietnam has to combine development based on export-led manufacturing with moving up the ladder of technology to skilled labour-intensive manufacturing and then to manufacturing based on advanced technology (Ishikawa 1998a, p. 15).

First, the government needs to identify and classify essential infant supportive industries, and focus its attention and resources to support the development of the infant industries that could be internationally competitive, with government protection for a certain period. As mentioned in chapter 5, such industries may include machinery, electronics, chemicals and petrochemicals.

Second, the protection of those infant industries should last for an appropriate period of time. The government should provide a schedule for tariff reduction for protected industries. This will give the producers enough time to prepare and at the same time expose those industries gradually to international competition. The year 2006 could be a suitable date for ending protection as, by that time, Vietnam will be fully integrated into the ASEAN Free Trade Area (AFTA) and complete all of its obligations to remove tariffs under AFTA's Common Effective Preferential Tariff scheme.

Third, the protection of those infant industries would be limited to a few measures in conformity with the requirements of international trade organizations such as WTO, AFTA or Asian Pacific Economic Co-operation (APEC). This process would include removing all non-tariff barriers such as export and import quotas, licences as well as other unnecessary customs requirements.

The gradual removal of protection for the domestic market and infant industries and the limiting of protection to only a few essential infant industries will lead to the refocusing of FDI flows toward export-oriented industries, improving the performance of FIEs and facilitating economic integration.

Economic integration

The government needs to consider FDI flows when Vietnam joins trading organizations such as AFTA, APEC and WTO. Policies relating to FDI promotion and co-ordination, therefore, need to be adjusted in accordance with the economic integration process in Vietnam, especially with Vietnam's commitment to removing tariffs under AFTA's common effective preferential tariff scheme. The content of Vietnam's commitment appears in Box 4.

There is a close link between economic integration and FDI flows (as mentioned in Chapter 2). For AFTA, the short-term purpose is to increase intra-ASEAN trade and the long-term purpose is to make ASEAN products more internationally competitive and hence, to make ASEAN more attractive to foreign investors. FDI flows since 1988 have promoted trade between Vietnam and the ASEAN countries. Several foreign investors, including those from ASEAN, have made use of Vietnam's cheap labour to produce exports for the ASEAN market.

Box 4
Vietnam's Commitment under AFTA Common Effective Preferential Tariff Scheme

Under the AFTA Common Effective Preferential Tariff scheme (CEPT), Vietnam has set out the tariff reduction schedule whose General Exception List includes 213 commodity groups, accounting for 6.6 percent of total commodity groups in its import tax list; the Temporary Exclusion List includes 1,317 commodity groups accounting for 40.9 percent of total commodity groups in import tax list while the Sensitive List includes 26 commodity groups, accounting for 0.8 percent of total commodity groups in the import tax list and the Inclusion List includes 1661 commodity groups, accounting for 51.6 percent of total commodity groups in import tax list (MOF 1999).

The determinant of those lists as well as the tariff reduction schedule reflect the government strategy of rapid tariff reduction for commodities that have high competitiveness (such as rice, coffee, tea, fishery products, textiles and garments, rubber) while delaying the tariff reduction in conformity with CEPT regulation for other industries. This strategy will provide protection for certain periods of time at a different extent for infant industries in order to help them to achieve a certain level of development before exposing them to international competition. Such infant industries include food processing, electrical and electronic items, mechanical, ship building, chemical, cement, metallurgy, minerals, paper and sugar industries. However, the tariff for those products will eventually reach 5 percent by 2006.

Source: MOF 1999.

In 1998, the ASEAN market had the biggest share of FIE exports. The cases of the Fujitsu joint venture producing personal computer accessories and Daewoo's joint venture producing television picture tubes for export to the international market, including ASEAN, are typical examples. In the automobile industry, three out of eleven joint-venture assembly cars and trucks in Vietnam imported components from ASEAN countries, though such imports still accounted for a low share of total imports (UNIDO and DSI 1999, pp. 165–9). However, the contribution of FDI flows in promoting trade between Vietnam and ASEAN is still insignificant.

While several studies have found that the integration of Vietnam into AFTA would provide from low to medium trade creation effects on exports and imports between Vietnam and ASEAN countries (Pham and Forbes 1996; Fukase and Martin 2001), the integration coupled with Vietnam's tariff reduction programme may have significant impact on FDI flows.

AFTA should lead to the restructuring of FDI flows between a number of countries in accordance with each country's comparative advantages. Especially for industries such as automobiles and electronics that have multiple processes, restructuring under AFTA would involve an intra-regional division of labour. As MNCs face labour shortages and rising wages in Singapore, Malaysia and Thailand, they could relocate their labour-intensive production processes to countries like Vietnam where labour is cheap and available. Mitsubishi Motor Corporation, for example, has decided to integrate Vietnam into its regional and local production and distribution network (Gates and Truong 1994, p. 25).

If MNCs relocate their production to Vietnam to make use of cheap labour and provide products for the whole ASEAN region, government policy to protect infant industries up until the year 2006 will provide favourable conditions to support this restructuring. The government should also provide preferential treatment (such as tax incentives) to promote FDI flows which create regional linkages.

Toward more equitable regional FDI allocation

The fifth policy implication is to adjust government incentives from providing tax incentives to improving the infrastructure in poorer provinces in order to improve their attractiveness to FDI, speeding up the diffusion of foreign investment outward from current centres and hence to achieve more equal regional distribution of FDI.

The result of the regression analysis in chapter 6 showed that the level of physical and social infrastructure (i.e. the number of telephones and the number of middle high school pupils per capita) has had decisive effects on the volume of FDI flows to each province: the better the infrastructure, the higher the FDI flows. On the other hand, the result also shows that tax incentives have had no effect in attracting FDI flows to poor and remote provinces.

This result underlines the necessity for the government to shift its concentration of public expenditure toward poorer, densely populated provinces located around big cities or less developed provinces or mountainous provinces with rich natural resources in order to improve their physical and social infrastructure. Only with significant improvements in infrastructure such as transportation, energy and water supplies as well as the quality of the labour force, will those poor provinces be able to attract larger amounts of foreign investment. Such improvement of infrastructure also helps to attract FDI flows into export-oriented industries that require better transport and telecommunications in order to respond effectively to the fluctuating demands of the international market.

With the diffusion of FDI flows toward poorer provinces as a result of infrastructure improvements, FDI flows would contribute more effectively and significantly to regional economic growth and reduce the gap between richer and poorer regions in Vietnam.

Conclusion

In conclusion, the examination of FDI flows in Vietnam over the 1988–98 period has led to several policy implications including the recognition of FDI as an important supplementary source of investment; the need for more concentration of FDI flows into export-oriented industries; the need to gradually reduce protection for infant industries; the need to recognize the close relations between FDI flows and economic integration; and the need for more equitable regional allocation of FDI flows. If such policies are implemented, they will make Vietnam more attractive and competitive to foreign investment and in turn make FDI flows more useful for economic growth and poverty alleviation, and hence for overall socio-economic development.

8
Conclusion

This chapter revisits the debates on FDI in the light of the data and analyses presented in this book.

As discussed in Chapter 1, the mainstream view argues that developing countries on the way to take-off are likely to face the four constraints of: the savings–investment, foreign exchange, fiscal, and skills and technology gaps. It suggests that FDI flows to developing countries will cover those gaps and hence promote economic growth. Furthermore, as FDI flows help cover these gaps, FDI will facilitate the industrialization process in developing countries, promote economic growth and, in the long run, contribute to the alleviation of poverty by generating employment and increasing income.

The radical view argues that FDI flows are the means by which developed countries extract profit from developing countries and keep poor countries in a state of underdevelopment. In particular, the radical view argues that FDI flows have contributed little to gross national investment and have decreased domestic savings by crowding out local entrepreneurs. Moreover, FDI flows also lead to a deterioration of the balance of payments as a consequence of the substantial importation of intermediate products and capital goods as well as the repatriation of profits, interests, royalties, and management fees. In addition, the contribution of multinationals to government budgets has been considerably less than it should have been as a result of tax concessions, subsidies and transfer pricing. Technology transfer under FDI flows, according to the radical view, is capital-intensive and not suitable for developing countries. These detrimental effects have been argued to have intensified with globalization.

The radical view concludes that FDI flows have not only failed to promote, but have in fact lowered, economic growth. The radical view also argues that FDI flows have actually exacerbated poverty in developing countries by negatively impacting on income distribution, failing to address unemployment and creating undesirable consumption patterns.

While the theoretical debates between mainstream and radical views on the role of FDI in socio-economic development are inconclusive, the examples and empirical evidence are also mixed. FDI flows have had a positive impact in some developing countries, especially the Asian newly industrialized countries (NICs), but generated many detrimental effects in other countries. The key to such inconclusive debates and mixed evidence may well lie in the role of government. Where a government follows a strategy of less direct intervention in the operation of foreign investors, minimizing operational and ownership requirements or providing incentives appropriate to the country's real conditions and generally creating a favourable environment, FDI flows tend to have fewer detrimental effects. In contrast, where a government follows a strategy of excessive direct intervention on the flow and operations of foreign investment, and implements import-substitution industrialization strategies, FDI tends to produce detrimental effects.

The experience of Central and Eastern European countries and the former Soviet Union in their transition towards a market economy shows that, where market institutions have not been fully established, government intervention is needed to guarantee the successful attraction and utilization of FDI. This seems to have been borne out in Vietnam, where the reforms towards a market-oriented economy in general, and government policies in particular, successfully attracted large amounts of committed and implemented FDI during the 1988–98 period. Government policies have also created the necessary conditions to maximize the useful contribution and minimize the detrimental effects of FDI flows on socio-economic development in Vietnam.

Over the 1988–98 period, about $35.3 billion of FDI was committed, of which $14.2 billion was implemented. Such large amounts of FDI commitment and implementation made Vietnam second in the world in terms of FDI as a percentage of GNP in 1996 (World Bank 1997a, p. 17). The large amount of FDI flows to Vietnam during this period has been mainly attributed to Vietnam's locational advantages of natural and human resources, a large local market, and the government's positive attitude toward foreign investment. On the other hand, other factors such as increasing labour costs in developed countries and internalization factors also contributed to the magnitude of FDI flows to Vietnam.

In general, FDI flows have had a significant impact on domestic savings and gross national investment, foreign exchange earnings and the national budget, and hence economic growth. FDI flows have contributed directly to gross national investment by bringing in important additional investment capital and indirectly by contributing to improvements in infrastructure, by generating backward effects. The analysis found no evidence that FDI flows have competed with state-owned enterprises (SOEs) or private enterprises and in fact there are several factors that promoted co-operation between them. FDI flows also contributed to foreign exchange earnings by their access to concessional credit sources, promoting export-oriented production through the provision of modern technology, capital and access to the international market. In 1998, exports generated by FDI flows accounted for over 21 percent of Vietnam's exports.

Foreign investment flows in Vietnam and their contribution to the budget over the 1988–98 period helped to cover the savings–investment, foreign exchange, and fiscal gaps and hence had a significant impact on GDP growth. The average contribution of FDI to GDP growth was between 1 to 1.5 percent over the 1993–98 period. FDI flows also contributed to economic growth in Vietnam by creating whole new industries or by significantly increasing the output of existing industries such as oil and gas, automobiles, electronics, garments, and steel.

In terms of technology transfer, FDI flows in Vietnam over the 1988–98 period brought with them modern technology, contributed to the production of new products and improvement in the quality of existing products and, in general, generated higher productivity. Moreover, FDI flows have also promoted industrial growth, facilitating the dual industrialization strategy of developing both export-oriented and import-substitution industries. FDI flows also contributed significant additional industrial capital—the average contribution of FIEs was about half of Vietnam's total industrial growth in the 1995–98 period.

The contribution of FDI flows to support export-oriented industries has been very significant. While only half of the actual FDI flows has been channelled to industries in which Vietnam has comparative advantages, FDI flows have contributed significantly to promoting the development of export-oriented industries through FIEs, which are the major factor behind the overall rise in export-oriented industries in Vietnam.

The other half of FDI into Vietnam has been channelled to import substitution industries and has played an important role in promoting the development of key infant supportive import-substitution industries by creating whole new industries or extending existing ones. Between 1994 and 1998, FDI contributed over 70 percent of the increasing capital of those industries but only 14 percent of the increasing output of those industries.

As far as regional development is concerned, FDI flows have concentrated in the Red River Delta and Southeast regions, especially in large cities like Ha Noi, Hai Phong and Ho Chi Minh City, though this imbalance improved in recent years as FDI started to diffuse to surrounding regions. The regression analysis on the factors influencing the provincial allocation of FDI flows between regions and provinces found that the level of infrastructure, the quality of the labour force and the size of local industry were all decisive in attracting foreign investment flows. Thus, although FDI flows have been unequally allocated between provinces and regions, they have contributed significantly to regional economies by providing additional capital and increasing each region's output.

The direct contribution of FDI flows to poverty alleviation has not been significant, however. The number of job places created by FDI flows accounted for under 1 percent of Vietnam's labour force and concentrated mainly in industrial areas, while nearly 80 percent of poor people work mainly in the agricultural sector. The main contribution of FDI flows to poverty alleviation in Vietnam has been indirectly through promoting rapid economic growth that, in turn, will create higher employment opportunity and income for the poor.

Overall, the significant contribution of FDI flows in Vietnam over the 1988–98 period has been attributed to the role of government policies. The government's policies on the one hand generated a relatively favourable environment for attracting foreign investment, but on the other hand, ensured that FDI generated positive impacts on the local economy through backward effects, technology transfer, and making use of Vietnam's comparative advantages of cheap and well educated labour. Several regression analyses have shown the importance of government policies such as tax preference and domestic protection policies on FIEs' performance.

The importance of government policies in attracting FDI and guaranteeing its positive contribution in Vietnam over the 1988–98 period also calls for several changes or adjustments. As discussed in Chapter 7, these policies need to be adjusted in order to make Vietnam an even more attractive destination for FDI within the region. Such changes and adjustments include the improvement of the legal and operational environment; greater concentration of FDI flows into export-oriented industries; gradually reducing protection for the domestic market and infant import-substitution industries; and achieving more equitable regional allocation of FDI flows. These amendments would remove several obstacles that have contributed to the slow-down of FDI flows into Vietnam since the late 1990s.

This examination of FDI flows in Vietnam over the 1988–98 period has illustrated the arguments put forward by both mainstream and radical analysts by showing the positive impacts, the limitations and the potential detrimental effects of FDI flows.

On the one hand, FDI's contribution to Vietnam's economic growth has supported the arguments of mainstream theorists such as Rostow (1963), Chenery and Strout (1966), Papanek (1973), Dowling and Hiemenz (1983) or the view of the World Bank (1997a) that FDI flows bring in supplementary capital and necessary modern technology and management skills.

On the other hand, radical theorists such as Frank (1969), Bornschier et al. (1978), London (1987, 1988), Boswell and Dixon (1990), Wimberley (1991) and Lewellen (1995) are right when criticizing FDI flows for failing to tackle the poverty problem directly. The FDI flows in Vietnam over the 1988–98 period did not generate a significant number of job places compared to SOEs or the private sector. Moreover, the disparity of allocation of FDI flows between provinces, between sectors, and between rural and urban areas, also worsened income inequality in Vietnam. Critics of FDI such as Frank (1969), Lall and Streeten (1997) are also correct when pointing out potential problems such as the crowding-out of local entrepreneurs, the outflow of foreign exchange, the transfer of inappropriate technology, or transfer pricing issues. These problems either have happened, or threaten to happen, in Vietnam.

Nevertheless, taken as a whole, the positive contributions of foreign direct investment over the 1988–98 period outweighs its detrimental effects. It has been widely accepted that Vietnam's successful attraction and effective utilization of FDI flows in the first decade of reform has been one of its most important achievements. Much of this success is due to government policies and intervention designed to promote the positive impact of FDI flows.

Summing up

The findings of this book support the arguments of Deyo (1987), Amsden (1989) and Wade (1991) that governments in developing countries have played a central and significant role in the socio-economic development process.

This book shows a positive picture of FDI flows in Vietnam and argues that government intervention was fairly successful in making use of FDI flows in Vietnam over the 1988–98 period. This may contradict the arguments of many western researchers who have focused on the difficulties of getting foreign invested projects operating in Vietnam or on the decline of FDI flows as a consequence of the regional financial crisis (World Bank 1999b; IMF 1999, Dixon 2000). These researchers have not paid much attention to the overall contribution of FDI flows to Vietnam's economy, the profits that foreign investors have received through investing in Vietnam, or the impact of government intervention on FDI flows. Such researchers have argued that the government of Vietnam needs to further liberalize the economy and limit government intervention and that Vietnam has forgone many advantages that FDI flows may bring to Vietnam if the economy was liberalized further. However, they forget to add that the detrimental effects of FDI flows may also have been greater without government intervention.

As Vietnam is in transition towards a market economy, government intervention is needed to attract and utilize FDI flows effectively and at the same time to maintain socio-economic stability, promote the development of local entrepreneurs, and tackle the poverty problem effectively.

The findings presented here also demonstrate that no single theory can be applied to analyzing the impact of FDI on socio-economic development; both mainstream or radical views can be a valid ways to explain the impact of FDI on development. To understand the contribution of FDI in developing countries requires a combination of several development theories. In addition, the role of government and the appropriateness of its intervention in the socio-economic development process needs to be taken into account. Nor is there a fixed format for government intervention: laissez-faire or centrally-planned systems may work for some countries but not for others. The practice of attracting and utilizing FDI flows in Asian NICs and in Vietnam reveals that only appropriate government intervention in accordance with the real development conditions of each country will guarantee the successful attraction and utilization of FDI flows.

While this book has examined several aspects of FDI flows in Vietnam, there are still several questions left unanswered which require further research. The Asian regional economic crisis that led to the reduction of foreign investment into Vietnam since 1997, and the strong reforms in neighbouring countries, have raised many questions for a government such as that of Vietnam as to which policies need to be changed to improve the investment environment. Further research is also needed in order to reduce the disparity of FDI allocation between regions and provinces, and between export-oriented and import-substitution industries. The operations, impact and problems of individual FDI projects are other aspects that lie beyond the scope of this book. Addressing these issues in combination with the findings of this book will provide lessons on how to make better use of FDI flows in economies in transition.

Appendix 1
Regression Analysis on Export Performance of Foreign Invested Enterprises, 1995–98

The model

In this regression analysis, the ratio of exports over revenue (ER) has been used to measure the export performance of FIEs. As mentioned in chapter 5, the export performance of the FIEs in primary (mainly mining) industry and manufacturing sectors has been argued to be influenced by government tax and domestic market protection policies, the share of foreign investors in FIEs' legal capital, the transfer of modern technology, and the country of origin of foreign investors.

As mentioned in chapter 2, tax incentives have played a very significant role in attracting FDI flows that focused on export-oriented industries. In fact, tax incentives may become an important determinant for export-oriented foreign investment decisions (Wells 1986; Gold 1991; Bishop 1997). In Vietnam, tax incentives have been used extensively to attract as well as promote such kinds of FDI flows. The impact of government tax policy on the export performance of FIEs—measured by the ratio of profit and revenue tax over revenue (TAX)—are that the lower the tax ratio, the higher the export performance.

Domestic market protection policies (PROTECT) are another government instrument to protect and promote the development of infant import-substitution industries. However, such policies may have adverse impacts on export performance as FIEs may find it is easier to produce for the lucrative protected local market than to export to the competitive international market. Details about domestic market protection policies have been discussed in chapter 5 and in Box 4.

The foreign share in legal capital (FOREIGN) may have a positive correlation with export performance as foreign investors have better knowledge of, and access to, the international market and 100 percent foreign-owned projects may be more export-oriented than joint ventures and BCCs. Technology transfer (TECH) may have either positive or negative impacts on export performance. It will have positive impacts if modern technology has been transferred to produce advanced products for exporting to the international market. However, if foreign investors intend to use cheap local labour to produce labour-intensive export products, then technology transfer will not play a decisive role in FIEs' export performance.

The country of origin of foreign investors (COUNTRY) may influence the export performance of FIEs. Kojima has argued that FDI that comes from Asian NICs and Japan tends to be export-oriented, while FDI from the United States, the European Union and ASEAN countries tends to be inward-oriented (Kojima 1978; 1991).

Based on those arguments, the export performance of FIEs will be the function of those variables as follow:

$$ER = f\ (PROTECT;\ FOREIGN;\ TAX;\ TECH;\ COUNTRY) \quad (1)$$

ER: Ratio of exports over revenue
PROTECT: Domestic market protection policies
FOREIGN: Foreign share in legal capital
TAX: Ratio of profit and revenue tax over revenue
TECH: Technology transfer
COUNTRY: Country of origin of foreign investors

Data

Data for the regression analysis have been selected for all FIEs in primary and manufacturing sectors in Vietnam, as they account for the majority of exports of foreign-invested projects. The data was collected and compiled through a quarterly survey of all FIEs by the pertinent ministries. The regression analysis focuses only on those FIEs with a record of profit or loss, as several FIEs in the survey data have not completed the start-up period.

Extensive data on the ratio of exports over revenue have been available only from 1996, and hence the regression analysis is used only for the 1996–98 period. The analysis covers only three years from 1996 to 1998, and therefore may not yet reflect fully the export performance of FIEs. Moreover, the 1996–98 period is also the period when committed and implemented FDI flows to Vietnam started to contract, largely as a consequence of the regional financial

138 *Foreign Direct Investment and Development in Vietnam*

crisis. However, the regression analysis of the period 1996–98 still reflects the impact of government policies on the export performance of the majority of FIEs. As FDI flows to Vietnam increased significantly between 1993 and 1996, a substantial proportion of those investment projects contained in the survey data had been in operation for more than two to three years.

Data on the ratio of tax over revenue are derived from the ratio of total revenue tax and profit tax over revenues for each project. The government domestic protection policies variable is a dummy variable, which is equal to one for protected products, and zero for unprotected products. The determination of this variable is based on the government's tariff reduction schedule under AFTA, and its Common Effective Preferential Tariff scheme. Products that belong to the general exception list, temporary exclusion list and the products of inclusion list, but which carry a high tariff rate of over 20 percent, will have a value equal to one, while other products on the inclusion list will be zero.

The data on the foreign equity share are based on the percentage contribution of foreign investors in the legal capital of FDI projects. The technology transfer variable is a dummy variable that is equal to one with projects that are registered as having technology transfer, and zero with projects that are not involved in technology transfer. The variable for "country of origin" is also a dummy variable and has been constructed for seven groups of country (or countries), based on the average ratio of exports over revenue for the 1991–98 period. The country that ranked lowest in terms of exports over revenue will have this variable equivalent to one, and the country that ranked highest is equivalent to seven. On that basis, this variable is equal to: one for FDI projects from the United States and Canada, two for FDI projects from Australia and New Zealand, three for FDI projects from ASEAN countries, four for FDI projects from the European Union, five for FDI projects from other countries, six for FDI projects from Japan and seven for FDI projects from Asian NICs.

Results

As there are no strong reasons to assume any other functional forms other than a linear relationship, a simple linear regression analysis is applied. Based on those data, the linear regression analysis has been tried to test the relationship between the export performance of FIEs and those explanatory variables for three years 1996, 1997 and 1998 when the data were available in sufficient number. The main results of the regression analysis are as follows:

1996
ER96 = –0.017 – 0.249 PROTECT* + 0.144 FOREIGN – 0.369 TAX***
    (0.053)   (–1.9)   (1.11)   (–2.85)

    – 0.062 TECH + 0.302 COUNTRY**
       (–0.48)   (2.32)

$\bar{R}^2$ = 0.253   D-W = 2.1 $F_{(5,41)}$ = 4.112***   SE = 0.40   N = 47

1997
ER97 = 0.126 – 0.291 PROTECT*** + 0.088 FOREIGN – 0.195 TAX***
    (0.765)   (–4.08)   (1.2)   (–2.72)

    – 0.087 TECH + 0.227 COUNTRY***
       (–1.19)   (3.13)

$\bar{R}^2$ = 0.171   D-W = 2.09 $F_{(5,158)}$ = 7.71***   SE = 0.4   N = 164

1998
ER98 = –0.263* – 0.303 PROTECT*** + 0.269 FOREIGN*** – 0.257 TAX***
    (–1.89)   (–5.04)   (4.49)   (–4.2)

    – 0.175 TECH*** + 0.279 COUNTRY***
       (–2.9)   (4.6)

$\bar{R}^2$ = 0.308   D-W = 1.98 $F_{(5,189)}$ = 18.296***   SE = 0.35   N = 195
***, ** and * indicates significant at 1, 5 and 10 percent level respectively. The figures in brackets are t-statistics.

In general, the tax ratio has a statistically significant (at the 1 percent level in 1996, 1997 and 1998) negative correlation with export performance of FIEs. This result means that the government tax incentives have a very strong impact on the export performance of FIEs. The lower the tax rate, the higher the export ratio. This result also supports the government's intensive use of tax incentives as means to attract FDI to develop export-oriented industries.

The domestic market protection policies also have a statistically significant (at the 1 percent level in 1997, 1998 and at the 10 percent level in 1996) negative correlation with the export performance of FIEs. This result implies that the higher the protection of the domestic market, the lower the export ratio of FIEs as they found that producing for the protected domestic market is easier than for the competitive international market.

The technology transfer has a negative correlation with the export performance of FIEs, though this was statistically significant at the 1 percent level only in 1998. This result implies that the production of export products in Vietnam has not yet used modern technology as, in the early stage, FDI flows were mainly involved in simple, labour-intensive and low value-added processing agriculture and light industry products for exports. While modern technology may not play a decisive role in producing export products in FIEs, their modern machinery and equipment and modern management methods have played important roles in the production of FIEs as mentioned in previous sections. Due to the problem of collecting and classifying data on technology transfer, the import of modern machinery and equipment and modern management methods have not been always recorded as technology transfer. Hence the result of the regression analysis has not reflected the role of modern machinery and equipment or modern management method in producing export products in FIEs.

The share of foreign contribution in a project's legal capital also has a positive correlation with export performance, though statistically significant at the 1 percent level in 1998. This may imply that the higher the share of foreign investors in projects' legal capital, the higher the export ratio. In other words, 100 percent foreign-owned enterprises may have a higher export ratio than other forms of FDI.

The dummy variable of country of origin of foreign investors also has a statistically significant (at the 1 percent level in 1997 and 1998 and at the 5 percent level in 1996) positive correlation with export performance. Based on the way of determining this dummy variable, the result supports the conclusion that the FDI projects with foreign investors coming from Asian NICs and Japan (which carry the highest dummy value of six and seven) have higher export ratios compared to other FDI projects. Once again, the Kojima hypothesis that Japanese FDI tends to be export-oriented while FDI flows from United States tend to be inward looking has been supported by the empirical evidence of FDI flows in Vietnam.

The correlation matrices show no multi-collinearity problem between independent variables except in 1997 between FOREIGN and TECH. However, the multi-collinearity test later shows no multi-collinearity problem as condition indices and collinearity statistics are within an acceptable range. In particular, the values of the variance inflation factor (VIF) are low for all independent variables.

The interpretation of this regression analysis must be carried out with care due to the low level of reliability of the data, and FIEs may have inflated their exports revenues in order to enjoy government tax incentives. Moreover, the export performance of FIEs in Vietnam has depended also on several factors that have not been included in this model, such as exchange rate changes in the international market. However, the high value of F-statistics for the three years 1996–98 means that those variables do have significant correlation with the export performance of FIEs.

Appendix 2
Regression Analysis on Foreign Invested Enterprises' Performance, 1998

The model

In general, the performance of FIEs has been measured by a profit ratio or profit over revenue (PROFIT). The higher the profit ratio, the better the performance of FIEs. Based on an analysis of the factors that explain FDI flows in Vietnam as well as government preferential policies to attract FDI flows to establish infant import-substitution industries, the performance of FIEs is expected to depend on the tax ratio, domestic market protection policies, the share of foreign contributions in projects' legal capital, the transfer of modern technology, the average wage of local workers and the time-span for projects in Vietnam.

As the government provides tax preferences to attract FDI flows, the tax ratio (TAX) seems to influence the profit ratio in the sense that the higher the tax rate, the lower the profit ratio. The domestic market protection policies (PROTECT), in contrast, protect FIEs from the competition of cheap imported products and hence make their operations more profitable. The more protection (through quotas, tariffs, local content requirements), the better the performance of FIEs. The share of foreign investors in projects' legal capital (FOREIGN) may have positive impacts for export-oriented industries, but little—or even negative—impacts on the performance of the projects, especially in import-substitution industries, as local partners may have better connections and knowledge about the domestic market. The transfer of technology (TECH) may have positive impacts on FIEs performance if their operation is capital-intensive and focuses on the local market, but no impact on FIEs that intend to make use of local cheap labour to produce export products. The average wage of local labour (WAGE) will influence the profit ratio in the sense that the lower the average wage, the higher the profit ratio. The time-span that the projects operate in Vietnam (YEAR), on the other hand, may influence the profit ratio in the sense that the longer they stay in a market, the better the knowledge of the market and connections they achieve and hence the higher the performance. Based on these arguments, the profit ratio of FIEs will be the function of those variables as follows:

PROFIT = f (TAX; PROTECT; FOREIGN; TECH; WAGE; YEAR) (2)

PROFIT: Profit ratio
TAX: Ratio of profit and revenue tax over revenue
PROTECT: Domestic market protection policies
FOREIGN: Foreign share in legal capital
TECH: Technology transfer
WAGE: Average wage of local labour
YEAR: The time that the projects operate in Vietnam

Data

The regression analysis is also limited to FDI projects in manufacturing and primary sectors as government policies and incentives have not had significant impact on FDI projects in the service sector. The determination of the tax ratio (TAX), domestic protection (PROTECT), the share of foreign investors in projects' legal capital (FOREIGN), and transfer of technology (TECH) is similar as to the formula 1. The data on average wages of local workers are based on the data that were collected and compiled through a quarterly survey of all FIEs by the pertinent ministries. The number of years that FIEs operate in Vietnam has been based on the report of the time when the projects started operating in Vietnam.[1] The determination of profit ratio has been based on the data on profit and revenue collected and compiled through a quarterly survey of all FIEs by the pertinent ministries. However, such data have been available in sufficient numbers only from 1995 up to 1998 and hence the regression analysis is used only for the 1995–98 period.

Results

As there are no strong reasons to assume any functional forms other than a linear relationship, a simple linear regression analysis has been tried for four years 1995, 1996, 1997 and 1998. However, the results of regression analysis for 1995, 1996 and 1997 are inconclusive as the values of adjusted R^2 are close to zero. Only in 1998, has the regression analysis provided a conclusive result as the number of observations involved in the regression analysis is the largest and the quality of reported data may be better than previous years. The major result of the 1998 regression analysis is as follows:

$$\text{PROFIT} = 0.102 + 0.14 \text{ PROTECT}^* - 0.139 \text{ FOREIGN}^{**} + 0.238 \text{ YEAR}^{***}$$
$$(0.19) \quad\quad (1.9) \quad\quad\quad (-2) \quad\quad\quad\quad (3.3)$$

$$- 0.544 \text{ TAX}^{***} - 0.018 \text{ TECH} - 0.012 \text{ WAGE}$$
$$(-7.9) \quad\quad\quad (-0.26) \quad\quad (-0.18)$$

$\bar{R}^2 = 0.358$ D-W = 2.0 $F_{(6,132)} = 13.8^{***}$ SE = 1.2   N = 139
***, ** and * indicates significant at the 1, 5 and 10 percent level respectively. The figures in brackets are t-statistics.

The 1998 regression analysis shows that the profit ratio of 139 FIEs (where the data are available), depends on government tax incentives, domestic market protection policies, the share of foreign investors in projects' legal capital, and on the number of years that projects have been operating for in Vietnam. The protection of the domestic market has a statistically significant (at the 10 percent level) positive correlation with profit ratios and implies that the higher the protection, the higher the profit. The share of foreign investors in projects' legal capital also has a statistically significant (at the 5 percent level), though negative, correlation, with profit ratio and implies that the higher the share of local partners, the higher the profit ratio. Another implication is that joint ventures have performed better than 100 percent foreign-owned projects in terms of profit making.

The number of years that projects operate in Vietnam also has a statistically significant (at the 10 percent level) positive correlation with the profit ratio, as expected. The longer the time FIEs operate in Vietnam, the better they understand local markets and government policies and the higher their profits. This result also explains the poor performance of FIEs in the early stages of operation. The tax incentives also have a statistically significant (at the 1 percent level) negative correlation with FIEs' profit ratio and this result implies that the higher the tax ratio, the lower the profit. This result also indicates that tax incentives still played an important role in attracting FDI flows, and in the performance of FIEs in Vietnam, at least in 1998. The technology transfer and average wage variables, however, do not have any statistically significant correlation with the profit ratio.

The correlation matrices show no multi-collinearity problem between independent variables except between YEAR and PROTECT. However, the multi-collinearity test later shows no multi-collinearity problem as condition indices and collinearity statistics are within the acceptable range. In particular, the values of the variance inflation factor (VIF) are low for all independent variables.

The interpretation of the result of this regression analysis, however, must take into consideration the low reliability levels of the data, especially the profit datas as FIEs may deflate their profits to avoid paying taxes. Also, there are several macroeconomic variables that have been omitted from the regression analysis such as the economic growth rate, inflation rate, and exchange rate.

Notes

[1] This may not be when projects start as it may take several years for projects to complete the construction cycle.

Appendix 3
Regression Analysis on Provincial Allocation of Foreign Direct Investment, 1988-98

The model

Several theories about the motivation for FDI flows have been discussed in Chapter 2 and those theories also create the foundation for extensive research on factors that influence the regional allocation of FDI flows within and between countries (Scaperlanda and Mauer 1969; Glickman and Woodward 1988; Hill and Munday 1991; Balcet 1997; Lecraw 1991; Wheeler and Mody 1992; Hill and Munday 1992; Friedman et al. 1992; Lucas 1993; Hennart and Park 1994; Lorre and Guisinger 1995; Buckley 1997; Mayer and Mucchielli 1998; Billington 1999; Coughlin and Segev 2000). Those researchers identify several factors that influence the regional allocation of FDI flows including market characteristics, government investment incentives, infrastructure and the labour force.

Market characteristics, or market size and growth in market size, have been found to influence FDI flows, especially inward-oriented FDI, in the sense that the larger the market size and the higher its growth rate, the larger the FDI flows. Several empirical studies have used income and income growth to represent market size and its growth and generally found income and income growth have statistically significant positive effects on FDI flows at both country and regional levels, for both developed and developing countries (Lecraw 1991; Wheeler and Mody 1992; Friedman et al. 1992; Hennart and Park 1994; Buckley 1997; Mayer and Mucchielli 1998; Billington 1999; Coughlin and Segev 2000). However, Lucas (1993, p. 402) has found a "weak positive correlation" between the size of domestic consumption spending and FDI flows in seven East and Southeast Asian countries—but FDI flows in those countries have been "somewhat responsive to incomes in major export markets". This reflects the domination of the outward-oriented nature of FDI flows in those countries.

Government investment incentives such as tax concessions, subsidies or tariff concessions are designed to attract FDI flows to host countries or focus FDI flows on targeted regions within a country. Several empirical studies have been carried out on investigating the influences of government incentives on regional allocation of FDI flows. Hill and Munday (1991, 1992) found that Regional Preferential Assistance had beneficial effects on FDI flows in the United Kingdom, while Friedman et al. (1992) also found that government promotion activities have influenced FDI flows to several states in the United States.

A large number of empirical studies have focused on the effectiveness of tax rates, especially corporate tax rates, on FDI flows. In order to maximize the marginal risk-adjust after-tax return, foreign investors may choose to invest in countries or regions with the lowest tax rates (Lorre and Guisinger 1995). In the studies by Friedman, Gerlowski and Silberman (1992), Lorre and Guisinger (1995), Mayer and Mucchielli (1998) and Billington (1999), tax rates have been found to be an important determinant of FDI flows in the United States, United Kingdom, US investment abroad or Japanese FDI in Europe.

Infrastructure is another factor that influences the allocation of FDI flows between and within countries. The general perception is that the better the infrastructure, the higher the level of FDI flows. However, the extent that infrastructure influences FDI flows depends on the special requirements of the industries in which inward-oriented FDI might be "more concerned" with infrastructure than outward-oriented FDI (Lorre and Guisinger 1995, pp. 296–8). Several factors have been used in empirical studies as a proxy of infrastructure to examine the influence of infrastructure on FDI flows, including kilometres of paved highways per capita, number of telephones and expenditure on road transport. Those studies have found that infrastructure plays a decisive role in attracting FDI flows in either developed or developing countries (Glickman and Woodward 1988; Leung 1990; Hill and Munday 1991, 1992; Wheeler and Mody 1992; Murphy 1992; Lorre and Guisinger 1995; Buckwalter 1995; Mucchielli 1998; Mayer and Billington 1999).

For developing countries, infrastructure is probably the most important determinant of FDI flows. As Wheeler and Mody (1992, p. 71) found that agglomeration benefits determine US investors' location decisions and among "agglomeration-related factors, infrastructure quality clearly dominates for developing economies". Several studies have found that major cities in many developing countries in Asia, Latin America and Eastern Europe with better infrastructure receive very large shares of total FDI flows (Leung 1990; Murphy 1992; Buckwalter 1995).

The labour force is also a very important determinant that may sway the investment location decisions of foreign investors as one of the major motivations of foreign investors to invest abroad is to look for a cheap labour force, especially in developing countries. The costs, availability and productivity of labour are the main factors that influence the pattern of regional allocation of FDI. Several empirical studies have found that the lower the labour costs, the higher the FDI flows in both developed and developing countries (Glickman and Woodward 1988; Lecraw 1991; Friedman et al. 1992; Mayer and Mucchielli 1998; Billington 1999; Coughlin and Segev 2000). Besides the costs of labour, productivity is another factor that may offset the high labour costs in attracting inward FDI flows as foreign investors look for not only cheap but also skilled labour. Productivity has been found to have a statistically significant positive correlation with FDI flows in the empirical studies by Friedman, Gerlowski and Silberman (1992) and Coughlin and Segev (2000), while Hill and Munday (1991) found labour cost per unit of labour has been negatively correlated with FDI. The availability of the labour force also influences patterns of regional allocation of FDI flows in the sense that "the more labour available locally, the more attractive the area is to foreign investors" (Billington 1999, p. 66). Friedman, Gerlowski and Silberman (1992) have found that unemployment rates (proxy of labour availability) have a positive correlation with FDI flows in the case of FDI in the United States.

In short, government investment incentives, market characteristics, labour force and infrastructure have been identified as major factors influencing the regional allocation of FDI flows within and between developed and developing countries.

In the case of Vietnam, the heavy concentration of FDI flows in the cities and provinces of the more developed Red River Delta and Southeast regions may also be attributed to the factors mentioned above, especially differences between provinces in terms of infrastructure conditions, a cheap and relatively well-educated labour force, fast growing local market and local economy, and government investment incentives.

The following section will use regression analysis to analyse how the level of infrastructure of each province, the size of the provincial market, the quality of the labour force of each province and the government incentives policy, influenced the allocation of FDI flows between provinces in Vietnam over the 1988–98 period.

In this regression analysis, the dependent variable will be the provincial allocation of committed FDI flows for the 1988–98 period and the provincial allocation of implemented FDI flows for the 1991–98 period (FDI) classified for 53 provinces.[1]

The first factor that influences the pattern of provincial allocation of FDI flows in Vietnam is the development of infrastructure. As far as infrastructure conditions are concerned, the level of infrastructure development has varied significantly between provinces in Vietnam. Transport conditions, energy and water supplies and telecommunications have been more developed in Ha Noi and Ho Chi Minh City as well as in provinces in the Red River Delta and Southeast regions compared to other regions and provinces, especially provinces in the Central Highlands and Mekong River Delta. The government policy of promoting the development of the three economic growth triangles has also led to a heavy concentration of public investment to improve infrastructure conditions in those already developed regions. During the 1996–98 period, 62.5 percent of total public expenditure was directed to those regions while the Northern Uplands and Central Highlands regions together received only 13 percent of total public expenditure.

In the present study, the independent variable that represents the development level of infrastructure in each province will be the average telephones per capita (TEL), as statistics on the level of transport, energy and water supplies for the 1988–98 period by province are not available. As the FDI flows may depend on the development level of infrastructure, it has been argued that the higher the number of telephones per capita, the higher the level of infrastructure and hence the higher the level of FDI flows.

The second factor is the cheap, but relatively well-educated, labour force of Vietnam. As mentioned in chapter 3, Vietnam's income per capita has been among the lowest of developing countries in Asia, but Vietnam's literacy and other social indicators are similar to those of lower middle income countries. The local labour force will be represented by two independent variables: the income per capita (INC) and the number of middle secondary school pupils per capita (PUP).

The income per capita of each province (INC) has been considered as the proxy of levels of wage rates in Vietnam as the use of the wage rate in a particular industry will not correctly represent the nature of the cost of the labour force in Vietnam. In this sense, the lower the income per capita, the higher the FDI flows.

The variable of the number of middle secondary school pupils per capita of each province (PUP) represents the quality of the labour force, as workers who completed the middle secondary school will more easily understand new technology and be able to better participate in industrial production. Moreover, the selection of the number of middle secondary school pupils instead of the literacy rate is due to the fact that Vietnam has attained a very high and even literacy rate among regions and provinces. Only the number of middle secondary school pupils will clearly show the difference in the quality of the labour force among regions and provinces. It is expected that FDI flows will be concentrated in provinces that have a higher quality labour force.

The third factor that may influence the regional allocation of FDI flows is the local market and its purchasing power. Chapter 4 has identified the fact that over the 1988–98 period, large amounts of FDI flows were channelled to several projects producing consumer products to meet increasing domestic demands. The income per capita variable (INC) also represents, to some extent, the capacity of the local market. In this case, the per capita income variable (INC) may have positive impacts on FDI flows as large amounts of FDI flows have been channelled to several projects producing consumer products to meet increasing domestic demands over the 1988–98 period.

The last factor is government policies—in this case, the government tax incentives provided to FDI projects invested in mountainous and remote areas as well as in areas with difficult natural, economic and social conditions as mentioned in the previous section. Besides government tax incentives, local government attitudes towards FDI have also influenced the pattern of regional allocation of FDI flows. In fact, the local authorities of some provinces (such as Ha Noi and Ho Chi Minh cities, Dong Nai and Song Be provinces) have provided more favourable conditions to foreign investors in terms of project appraisal and approval compared to other provinces. While such incentives provided by local authorities have contributed to attracting large amounts of FDI flows to those provinces, they are very difficult to quantify and therefore this regression analysis will focus only on government tax incentives.

The independent variable representing government tax incentives (TAX) is the average tax ratio, calculated based on the ratio of turnover tax and profit tax over total turnover of FDI projects classified by 53 provinces. It is expected that FDI projects in mountainous and remote provinces will have a lower tax ratio than that of FDI projects in other provinces.

Based on the above argument, the provincial allocation of FDI flows will be the function of the following independent variables:

$$FDI = f\ (TEL;\ INC;\ PUP;\ TAX) \qquad (3)$$

FDI: provincial allocation of committed FDI flows for the 1988–98 period (or implemented FDI flows for the 1991–98 period).
TEL: average telephones per capita of each province
INC: income per capita of each province
PUP: number of middle secondary school pupil of each province
TAX: tax ratio of total FDI projects of each province

Data

The data for the dependent variable of provincial FDI flows will include two sets of data: the data of total committed FDI flows to each province for the 1988–98 period from the 1998 *Statistical Yearbook* (GSO 1999) and the data of total implemented FDI flows to each province for the 1991–98 period from the database that was collected and compiled through a quarterly survey of all FIEs by pertinent ministries. The data for independent variables should ideally be the average data for the 1988–98 period. However, due to the lack of data, the data for independent variables have been chosen for the year in the middle of the 1988–98 period when the data were available in order to represent closely the impacts of those variables during the whole period. While those data may not reflect the true meaning of those independent variables, they still represent the impacts of those independent variables on FDI flows in Vietnam during the 1988–98 period.

The data on the number of telephones per capita of each province are for 1995 when the data were first available. There may be a problem of inter-relation between FDI flows and the number of telephones per capita as FDI flows may contribute to improving the local telecommunication networks. However, the data on the number of telephone per capita of each province in 1995 have not been influenced by FDI flows, since FDI flows to Vietnam before 1995 focused mainly on developing the international communication networks.

The data on the number of middle secondary school pupils per capita of each province are for 1998 when those data were first available. Those data come from the 1998's statistical yearbooks. The data on income per capita of each province come from the 1993 Vietnam living standard survey and the data on average tax ratios have been calculated for the 1991–98 period based on the database collected and compiled through a quarterly survey of all FIEs by the pertinent ministries.

The data on the provincial allocation of committed and implemented FDI flows as well as other data, show a very large gap between more developed provinces and provinces in remote and mountainous areas. The amount of committed and implemented FDI flows in Ha Noi and Ho Chi Minh cities are a thousand times higher than those for mountainous provinces. Due to these distributional properties, all variables in this regression analysis are logged. Under this logarithm form, formula 6.1 will be rewritten as follow:

$$LnFDI = f\ (LnTEL;\ LnINC;\ LnPUP;\ LnTAX) \qquad (4)$$

However, as some provinces record zero for some variables such as committed and implemented FDI flows or TAX, those observations will be excluded when they are transferred into logarithm form and hence reduce the number of observations for the regression analysis. In order to avoid this problem, a small value of 0.01 will be added to each observation when it is being transformed into logarithm form.[2]

Results

Based on those data, a simple linear regression analysis is applied as a linear relationship is assumed since there are no strong reasons to assume any other functional form. The main results of regression analysis are as follows:

For committed FDI flows over the 1988–98 period:
$$LnFDI = 10.55 + 0.44\ LnTEL^{***} + 0.23\ LnINC^{*} + 0.32\ LnPUP^{***} + 0.16\ LnTAX$$
$$(1.53) \quad (3.4) \quad (1.74) \quad (3.2) \quad (1.4)$$

$\bar{R}^2 = 0.517 \quad D\text{-}W = 1.76 \quad F_{(4, 48)} = 14.9^{***} \quad SE = 1.26 \quad N = 53$

For implemented FDI flows over the 1991–98 period:
$$LnFDI = 1.34 + 0.3\ LnTEL^{**} + 0.35\ LnINC^{**} + 0.25\ LnPUP^{**} + 0.23\ LnTAX^{**}$$
$$(0.22) \quad (2.34) \quad (2.63) \quad (2.51) \quad (2.07)$$

$\bar{R}^2 = 0.528 \quad D\text{-}W = 1.88 \quad F_{(4, 48)} = 15.5^{***} \quad SE = 1.1 \quad N = 53$

***, ** and * indicates significant at 1, 5 and 10 percent level respectively. The figures in brackets are the t-statistic.

In general, the results of the regression analysis support the above arguments on the factors which influence the provincial allocation of FDI flows in Vietnam. The results of both regression analyses for committed and implemented FDI flows show that the number of telephones per capita of each province is positively correlated with FDI flows, statistically significant at the 1 percent level in the case of committed FDI flows and at the 5 percent level in the case of implemented FDI flows. The results imply that the level of infrastructure of each province has decisive effects on the volume of FDI flows and that the better the infrastructure, the higher the FDI flows. This result explains the reasons why a large amount of FDI flows have been committed or channelled to the few largest cities that have better transport, telecommunication, energy and water supply conditions.

The positive correlation of income per capita to implemented FDI flows and committed FDI flows (statistically significant at the 5 percent and 10 percent levels respectively) may not mean the higher the wages, the larger the FDI flows. Such positive correlation of income per capita may, in fact, imply that the higher the income, the more lucrative the local market and hence the more attractive it is to FDI flows.

The number of middle secondary school pupils also has a positive correlation with FDI flows though statistically significant at the 1 percent level in the case of committed FDI flows and at the 5 percent level in the case of implemented FDI flows. This result implies that the quality of the labour force of each province has played a decisive role in attracting

FDI flows. The large cities and more developed provinces with a well-educated labour force have, therefore, attracted large amounts of FDI flows.

The tax ratio has a statistically significant (at the 5 percent level) positive correlation with implemented FDI flows, but it is not statistically significant in the case of committed FDI flows. This result may imply that the government tax incentives have not provided any significant effects on attracting committed FDI flows as well as implementing committed FDI projects in mountainous or remote provinces. This result coincides with the fact that remote and mountainous provinces have received very small amounts of FDI flows compared to more developed provinces and cities, even though the government has offered tax incentives for FDI projects in those provinces.

There may be a multi-collinearity problem between some independent variables, for example, high incomes may lead to a high number of telephones per capita or a larger local market. However, the multi-collinearity test later shows no multi-collinearity problem as the values of variance inflation factor (VIF) for all independent variables are low and within an acceptable range. The condition indices are high but they are not likely to indicate multi-collinearity between independent variables. In fact, the high value of condition indices indicates the low value of independent variables and their close relation with the constant.

Notes

[1] Since 1996, the number of provinces in Vietnam has been 61. However, as the statistical data for the 1988–98 period have been collected based on the old administrative system of 53 provinces, the data for this regression analysis has been based on 53 provinces.

[2] $LnFDI = Ln(FDI + 0.01)$
$LnTEL = Ln(TEL + 0.01)$
$LnINC = Ln(INC + 0.01)$
$LnPUP = Ln(PUP + 0.01)$
$LnTAX = Ln(TAX + 0.01)$

Bibliography

Adjubei, Y. "Foreign Investment in the Commonwealth of Independent States: Growth, Operations and Problems". In *Foreign Investment in Central and Eastern Europe*, edited by P. Artisien, M. Rojec and M. Svetlicic, pp. 85–108. New York: St. Martin's Press, 1993.

Agodo, O. "The Determinants of US Private Manufacturing Investments in Africa". *Journal of International Business Studies* 9, no. 3 (1978): 95–107.

Ahiakpor, J. *Multinationals and Economic Development: An Integration of Competing Theories*. London: Routledge, 1990.

Aliber, R.Z. "Transfer Pricing: A Taxonomy of Impacts on Economic Welfare". In *Transnational Corporations and Regional Economic Integration*, edited by P. Robson, pp. 40–52. London: Routledge, 1993.

Amin, S. *Imperialism and Unequal Development*. New York: Monthly Review Press, 1977.

Amsden, A.H. *Asia's Next Giant: South Korea and Late Industrialisation*. New York: Oxford University Press, 1989.

Aristotelous, K. and S. Fountas. "An Empirical Analysis of Inward Foreign Direct Investment Flows in the EU with Emphasis on the Market Enlargement Hypothesis", *Journal of Common Market Studies* 34 (1996): 571–83.

Bacha, E.L. "A Three-Gap Model of Foreign Transfers and the GDP Growth Rate in Developing Countries". *Journal of Development Economics* 32 (1990): 279–96.

Balasubramanyam, V.N. and M.A. Salisu. "Export Promotion, Import Substitution and Direct Foreign Investment in Less Developed Countries". In *International Trade and Global Development: Essays in Honour of Jagdish Bhagwati*, edited by A. Koekkoek and L.B.M. Mennes, pp. 191–210. London: Routledge, 1991.

Balasubramanyam, V.N. and D. Greenaway. "Regional Integration Agreements and Foreign Direct Investment". In *Regional Integration and the Global Trading System*, edited by K. Anderson and R. Blackhurst, pp. 147–66. New York: St. Martin's Press, 1993.

Balcet, G. "International relocation strategies of Italian firms". In *Multinational Firms and International Relocation*, edited by P.J. Buckley and J.L. Mucchielli, pp. 71–89. Cheltenham, U.K.: Brookfield, 1997.

Baran, P. *The Political Economy of Growth*. New York: Monthly Review Press, 1957.

Barz, M. "British and German MNCs in Russia and the FSU: Evidence from the Western Side". In *Foreign Direct Investment and Technology Transfer in the Former Soviet Union*, edited by D.A. Dyker, pp. 102–54. Northampton, M.A.: Edward Elgar, 1999.

Bezanson, K., J. Annerstedt, K.M. Chung, D. Hopper, G. Oldham and F. Sagasti. *Vietnam at the Crossroads: The Role of Science and Technology*. Toronto: International Development Research Centre, 1999.

Bich N. "Black Viet Kieu Business Costing the Budget Dear". *Vietnam Investment Review*, no. 385 (1999a).

———. "Largest Sugar Cane Plant Secures Jobs". *Vietnam Investment Review*, no. 380 (1999b).

Biersteker, T. *Distortion or Development: Contending Perspectives on the Multinational Corporation*. Cambridge, Mass.: MIT Press, 1978.

Billington, N. 1999, "The Location of Foreign Direct Investment: An Empirical Analysis". *Applied Economics 31* (1999): 65–76.

Bishop, B. *Foreign Direct Investment in Korea: The Role of the State*. Brookfield, Vt.: Ashgate, 1997.

Blomström, M. and H. Persson. "Foreign Investment and Spillover Efficiency in an Underdeveloped Economy: Evidence from the Mexican Manufacturing Industry". *World Development 11*, no. 6 (1983): 493–501.

Blomström, M., R. Lipsey and M. Zejan. "What Explains Developing Country Growth". *NBER Working Paper 4132*. Cambridge: Mass., 1992.

Bornschier, V. and C. Chase-Dunn. "Reply to Szymanski". *American Journal of Sociology 89*, no. 3 (1983): 694–9.

Bornschier, V., C. Chase-Dunn and R. Rubinson. "Cross-national Evidence of the Effects of Foreign Investment and Aid on Economic Growth and Inequality: A Survey of Findings and Reanalysis". *American Journal of Sociology 84*, no. 3 (1978): 651–83.

Borensztein, E., J. De Gregorio and J.-W. Lee. "How does Foreign Direct Investment Affect Economic Growth", NBER Working Paper 5057. Cambridge, Mass., 1995.

Bos, H. Cornelis, M. Sanders and C. Secchi. *Private Foreign Investment in Developing Countries*. Dordrecht: D. Reidel Publishing Company, 1974.

Boswell, T. and W.J. Dixon. "Dependency and Rebellion: A Cross-National Analysis". *American Sociological Review 55* (1990): 540–9.

Brewer, A. *Marxist Theories of Imperialism*. London: Routledge and Kegan Paul, 1980.

Buckley, P.J. "Multinational Firm Strategies and the Impact of the Location Decisions". In *Multinational Firms and International Relocation*, edited by P.J. Buckley and J.L. Mucchielli, pp. 34–51. Cheltenham, U.K.; Brookfield, Vt., US: Edward Elgar 1997.

Buckwalter, D.W. "Spatial Inequality, Foreign Investment, and Economic Transition in Bulgaria". *Professional Geographer 47*, no. 3 (1995): 288–98.

Cadroso, E.A. and R. Dornbusch. "Foreign Private Capital Flows". In *Handbook of Development Economics*, Vol. 2, edited by H. Chenery and T.N. Srinivasan, pp. 1387–440. Amsterdam: North Holland, 1989.

Calderon, A., M. Mortimore and W. Peres. "Mexico: Foreign Investment as a Source of International Competitiveness". In *Foreign Direct Investment and Governments: Catalysts for Economic Restructuring*, edited by J.H. Dunning and R. Narula, pp. 240–79. New York: Routledge, 1996.

Cardoso, F.H. "Dependency and Development in Latin America". *New Left Review*, no. 70 (1972): 83–95.

Cassen, R. *Does Aid Work?* New York: Routledge, 1986.

Caves, R. *Multinational Enterprise and Economic Analysis*. New York: Cambridge University Press, 1982.

Chen, C. "The Impacts of FDI and Trade". In *Foreign Direct Investment and Economic Growth in China*, edited by Y. Wu, pp. 71–99. Cheltenham, U.K.: Edward Elgar, 1999.

Chen, E.K.Y. "Foreign Direct Investment in Asia Developing Country Versus Developed Country Firms". In *Transnational Corporations and Technology Transfer to Developing Countries*, edited by E.K.Y. Chen, pp. 381–405. New York: Routledge, 1990.

——. "Foreign Direct Investment in East Asia". *Asian Development Review 11*, no. 1 (1993): 24–59.

——, (ed.). *Transnational Corporations and Technology Transfer to Developing Countries*. New York: Routledge, 1994.

Chenery, H.B. and N.G. Carter. "Foreign Assistance and Development Performance, 1960–1970". *American Economic Association 63*, no. 2 (1973): 459–68.

Chenery, H.B. and A.M. Strout. "Foreign Assistance and Economic Development". *American Economic Review 56* (1966): 680–733.

Coughlin, C.C. and E. Segev. "Foreign Direct Investment in China: A Spatial Econometric Study". *The World Economy 23*, no. 1 (2000): 1–23.

DeMelo, J.D., A. Panagariya and D. Rodrik. "The New Regionalism: A Country Perspective". In *New Dimensions in Regional Integration*, edited by J.D. DeMelo and A. Panagariya, pp. 159–201. Cambridge: Cambridge University Press, 1992.

Deyo, F. *The Political Economy of East Asian Industrialism*. Ithaca: Cornell University Press, 1987.
Dixon, C. "State Versus capital: The Regulation of the Vietnamese Foreign Sector". *Singapore Journal of Tropical Geography 21*, no. 3 (2000): 279–94.
Do, Q.S. "Socio-Economic Development Policy and Investment and Co-operation with Foreign Countries". *Tap Chi Nghien Cuu Ly Luan* [Journal of Theoretical Research], no. 8 (1996): 1–8.
Dos Santos, T. "The Structure of Dependence". *American Economic Review* 60 (1970): 231–6.
Dowling, J.M. and U. Hiemenz. "Aid, Savings and Growth in the Asian Region". *Developing Economies 21*, no. 1 (1983): 3–13.
Duc H. "Honda Your Bikes, Yamaha Tell Rivals". *Vietnam Investment Review*, no. 330 (1998).
Dunning, J.H. "The Prospects for Foreign Direct Investment in Eastern Europe". In *Foreign Investment in Central and Eastern Europe*, edited by P. Artisien, M. Rojec and M. Svetlicic, pp. 16–33. New York: St. Martin's Press, 1993.
Dunning, J.H. and R. Narula. "The Investment Development Path Revisited: Some Emerging Issues". In *Foreign Direct Investment and Governments: Catalysts for Economic Restructuring*, edited by J.H. Dunning and R. Narula, pp. 1–41. New York: Routledge, 1996.
Dutt, A.K. "Direct Foreign Investment, Transnational Corporations and Growth: Some Empirical Evidence and a North-South Model". In *Transnational Corporations and the Global Economy*, R. Kozul-Wright and R. Rowthorn, pp. 164–94. New York: St. Martin Press, 1998.
Dyker, D.A. *Foreign Direct Investment and Technology Transfer in the Former Soviet Union*. Northampton M.A.: Edward Elgar, 1999.
Ebashi, M., H. Sakai and N. Takada. "Development Policy on SMEs and Supporting Industries in Vietnam". In *Study on Economic Development Policy in the Transition Toward a Market-oriented Economy in Vietnam—Phase 2*, Ministry of Planning and Investment of the Socialist Republic of Vietnam (MPI) and Japan International Co-operation Agency (JICA) 2, pp. 49–56. Hanoi, 1998.
Economist. "When War and Trade Don't Mix". *Economist*, 19 December (1987): 25.
Elson, D. "Dominance and Dependency in the World Economy". In *Survival and Change in the Third World*, edited by B. Crow and M. Thorpe, pp. 264–87. Cambridge: Polity/Open University Press, 1998.
Fforde, A. and S. deVylder. *From Plan to Market—The Economic Transition in Vietnam*. Boulder: Westview Press, 1996.
Frank, A.G. "The Development of Underdevelopment". *Monthly Review 18*, no. 4 (1966): 17–31.

―――. *Latin America: Underdevelopment or Revolution?* New York: Monthly Review Press, 1969.

Friedman, J., Gerlowski D. and Silberman J. "What Attracts Foreign Multinational Corporations? Evidence from Branch Plant Location in the United States". *Journal of Regional Science 32*, no. 4 (1992): 403–18.

Frischtak, C.R. and R.S. Newfarmer. "Market Structure and Industrial Performance". In *Transnational Corporations and World Development*. United Nations Conference on Trade and Development (UNCTAD), pp. 294–326. New York: Thomson Press, 1996.

Fry, M.J. "Foreign Direct Investment in East Asia". In *Lessons From East Asia*, edited by D.M. Leipziger, pp. 511–40. Ann Arbor: Michigan University Press, 1997.

Fukase, E. and W. Martin. "Free Trade Area Membership as a Stepping Stone to Development: The Case of ASEAN". World Bank Discussion Paper, Washington D.C.: World Bank, 2001.

Fukui, K. "Policy alternatives and Their Implications for Capital Intensive and Infant Industries". In *Study on Economic Development Policy in the Transition Toward a Market-oriented Economy in Vietnam—Phase 2*, Ministry of Planning and Investment of the Socialist Republic of Vietnam (MPI) and Japan International Co-operation Agency (JICA) 2, pp. 33–48. Hanoi, 1998.

Gates, C. and D. Truong. *Foreign Direct Investment and Economic Change in Vietnam—Trends, Causes and Effects*. Copenhagen: Nordic Institute of Asian Studies, 1994.

General Statistical Office (GSO). *Projection of Population, School Enrolment and Labour Force of Vietnam 1990–2005*. Hanoi: Statistical Publishing House, 1994.

―――. *Vietnam—Trade in the Open Door Time*. Hanoi: Statistical Publishing House, 1996.

―――. *Major Social and Economic Information Obtained from the Largest Surveys in the Period of 1990–1996*. Hanoi: Statistical Publishing House, 1998.

―――. *Results of the Survey on State-Owned Trade and Service Companies and Foreign Investment Trade and Service Companies*. Hanoi: Statistical Publishing House, 1999a.

―――. *Statistical Yearbook 1998*. Hanoi: Statistical Publishing House, 1999b.

―――. *Results of 1998 Industrial Survey*. Hanoi: Statistical Publishing House, 1999c.

―――. *Statistical Yearbook 1999*. Hanoi: Statistical Publishing House, 2000.

Gillis, M., D. Perkins, M. Roemer and D. Snodgrass. *Economics of Development*, 3rd edition. New York: W.W. Norton and Co, 1992.

Glickman, N.J. and D.P. Woodward. 1988, "The Location of Foreign Direct Investment in the United States: Pattern and Determinants". *International Regional Science Review 11*, no. 2 (1988): 137–54.

Gold, D. "The Determinants of FDI and their Implications for Host Developing Countries". *The CTC Reporter*, no. 31 (1991): 21–4.

Government of Vietnam (GOV) and the World Bank. *Vietnam Attacking Poverty*. Hanoi, 1999.

Graham, E.M. and P.R. Krugman. "The Surge in Foreign Direct Investment in the 1980s". In *Foreign Direct Investment*, edited by A.F. Kenneth, pp. 1–20. Chicago: University of Chicago Press, 1993.

Gupta, Kanhaya and Anisul Islam. *Foreign Capital, Savings and Growth*. Boston: Riedel, 1983.

Ha Thang. "Change the Attitude to Role of FDI". *Vietnam Investment Review*, no. 431 (2000): 12.

Hagiu, K., T. Kiuchi, S. Aoyama and M. Matsumoto. "Study on the Current Conditions of Production, Management and Finance of the State Owned Enterprises in Vietnam In *Study on Economic Development Policy in the Transition Toward a Market-oriented Economy in Vietnam—Phase 2*, Ministry of Planning and Investment of the Socialist Republic of Vietnam (MPI) and Japan International Co-operation Agency (JICA) 4, pp. 111–204. Hanoi, 1998.

Harvie, C. and Van H.T. *Vietnam's Reform and Economic Growth*. London: Macmillan, 1997.

Helleiner, G.K. "Transnational Corporations and Direct Foreign Investment". In *Handbook of Development Economics*, Vol. 2, edited by H. Chenery and T.N. Srinivasan, pp. 144–80. Amsterdam: North Holland, 1989.

——. "Direct Foreign Investments and Manufacturing for Export in Developing Countries: A Review of the Issues". In *Foreign Direct Investments*, edited by H.W. Singer, N. Hatti and R. Tandon, pp. 139–70. New Delhi: Indus Publishing Company, 1991.

Hennart, J.F. and Y.R. Park. "Location, Governance and Strategic Determinants of Japanese Manufacturing Investment in the US". *Strategic Management Journal 15*, (1994): 419–36.

Hill, H. and B. Johns. "The Role of Direct Foreign Investment in Developing East Asian Countries". In *Foreign Direct Investments*, edited by H.W. Singer, Hatti N. and R. Tandon, pp. 259–80. New Delhi: Indus Publishing Company, 1991.

Hill, S. and M. Munday. "The Determinants of Inward Investment: A Welsh Analysis". *Applied Economics 23*, no. 11 (1991): 1761–9.

Hill, S. and M. Munday. "The UK Regional Distribution of Foreign Direct Investment: Analysis and Determinants". *Regional Studies 26*, no. 6 (1992): 535–44.

Hogendorn, J.S. "Foreign private investment". In *Development Studies—An Introduction Through Selected Readings*, edited by R. Ayres, pp. 414–32. Kent: Greenwich University Press, 1995.

Hymer, S.H. "The International Operations of National Firms: A Study of Direct Foreign Investment", Ph.D. dissertation: Massachusetts Institute of Technology, 1960.

Imada, P., M. Montes and S. Naya. *A Free Trade Area—Implications for ASEAN*. Singapore: Institute of Southeast Asian Studies, 1991.

International Monetary Fund (IMF). *Vietnam Transition to a Market Economy*. Washington D.C: IMF, 1996.

——. *Vietnam—Selected Issues*. Washington D.C.: IMF, 1999.

Ishikawa, S. "Introduction". In *Study on Economic Development Policy in the Transition Toward a Market-oriented Economy in Vietnam—Phase 2*, Ministry of Planning and Investment of the Socialist Republic of Vietnam (MPI) and Japan International Co-operation Agency (JICA) 1, pp. 3–28. Hanoi, 1998a.

——. "Vietnam Participation in Economic Organisations: Japan's Experiences". In *Study on Economic Development Policy in the Transition Toward a Market-oriented Economy in Vietnam—Phase 2*, Ministry of Planning and Investment of the Socialist Republic of Vietnam (MPI) and Japan International Co-operation Agency (JICA) 1, pp.: 3–28. Hanoi, 1998b.

Jenkins, R. *Transnational Corporations and Uneven Development: the Internationalisation of Capital and the Third World*. New York: Methuen, 1987.

Katseli, L. *Foreign Investment and Trade Interlinkages in the 1990s: Experience and Prospects of Developing Countries*. London: Centre For Economic Policy Research, 1992.

Kojima, K. *Direct Foreign Investment—A Japanese Model of Multinational Business Operations*. London: Croom Helm, 1978.

——. "Japanese and American Direct Investment in Asia: A Comprehensive Analysis". In *Foreign Direct Investments*, edited by Singer, H.W., N. Hatti and R. Tandon, pp. 399–436. New Delhi: Indus Publishing Company, 1991.

Korten, D. *When Corporations Rule the World*. West Hartford, Conn.: Kumarian Press, 1995.

Lall, S. and P. Streeten. *Foreign Investment, Transnationals and Developing Countries*. New York: Macmillan, 1977.

Lao Dong "News brief". *Lao Dong*, 25 May 2000.

Lawrence, R. *Regionalism, Multilateralism, and Deeper Integration*. Washington D.C.: The Brookings Institution, 1996.

Le, D.D. "Foreign Investment and the Macro-Economy in Vietnam". In *Economic Development and Prospects in the ASEAN—Foreign Investment and Growth in Vietnam, Thailand, Indonesia and Malaysia*, edited by Tran Van Hoa, pp. 44–86. Basingstoke: Macmillan, 1997.

Le, D.D. and T.C. Tran. "The SOEs Reform Policies in Vietnam and their Implication Performance". In *Study on Economic Development Policy in the Transition Toward a Market-Oriented Economy in Vietnam—Phase 2*. Ministry of Planning and Investment of the Socialist Republic of Vietnam (MPI) and Japan International Co-operation Agency (JICA) 4, pp. 19–50. Hanoi, 1988.

Lecraw, D.J. "Factors Influencing FDI by TNCs in Host Developing Countries: A Preliminary Report". In *Multinational Enterprises in Less Developed Countries*, edited by P.J. Buckley and J. Clegg, pp. 163–80. Basingstoke: Macmillan, 1991.

———. "Indonesia: The Critical Role of Government". In *Foreign Direct Investment and Governments: Catalysts for Economic Restructuring*, edited by J.H. Dunning and R. Narula, pp. 316–47. New York: Routledge, 1996.

Lee, C.H. "Direct Foreign Investment and the Economic Development of Korea". In *Economic Development in East and Southeast Asia: Essays in Honour of Professor Shinichi Ichimura*, edited by S. Naya and A. Takayama, pp. 169–84. Singapore: Institute of Southeast Asian Studies, 1990.

Leung, C.K. "Locational Characteristics of Foreign Equity Joint-Venture Investment in China, 1979–1985". *Professional Geographer 42*, no. 4 (1990): 403–21.

Lewellen, T. *Dependency and Development: An Introduction to the Third World*. Westport, Conn.: Bergin and Garvey, 1995.

Lim, D. "Fiscal Incentives and Direct Foreign Investment in Less Developed Countries". *Journal of Development Studies* 19, no. 2 (1982): 207–12.

Lim, L.Y.C. and Pang E.F. *Foreign Direct Investment and Industrialisation in Malaysia, Singapore, Taiwan and Thailand*. Paris: OECD, 1991.

Lim, D. "Explaining the Growth Performance of Asian Developing Economies". *Economic Development and Cultural Change* 42, no. 4 (1994): 829–44.

Lindblad, T. *Foreign Investment in Southeast Asia in the Twentieth Century*. New York: St. Martin's Press, 1997.

London, B. "Structural Determinants of Third World Urban Change: An Ecological and Political Economic Analysis". *American Sociological Review* 52, (1987): 28–43.

———. "Dependence, Distorted Development, and Fertility Trends in Non-Core Nations: A Structural Analysis of Cross-National Data". *American Sociological Review* 53, (1988): 606–18.

London, B. and T.D. Robinson. "The Effect of International Dependence on Income Inequality and Political Violence". *American Sociological Review 54* (1989): 305–8.

―――― and D.A. Smith. "Urban Bias, Dependence, and Economic Stagnation in Non-Core Nations". *American Sociological Review* 53 (1988): 454–63.

―――― and B.A. Williams. "Multinational Corporate Penetration, Protest, and Basic Needs Provision in Non-Core Nations: A Cross-National Analysis". *Social Forces* 66 (1988): 747–73.

―――― and B.A. Williams. "National Politics, International Dependency, and Basic Needs Provision: A Cross-National Study". *Social Forces* 69 (1990): 565–84.

Lorre, D.W. and S.E. Guisinger. "Policy and Non-Policy Determinants of U.S. Equity Foreign Investment". *Journal of International Business Studies* 26, no. 2 (1995): 281–99.

Lucas, R.E.B. "On the Determinants of Direct Foreign Investment: Evidence from East and Southeast Asia". *World Development* 21, no. 3 (1993): 391–406.

Luu, Q.D. "Just Do It and Forget about Target". *Lao Dong*, 16 June, 2000.

Luu, V.D. "Foreign Investment Law in Vietnam: Legal and Economic Aspects and Comparative Analysis". In *Economic Development and Prospects in the ASEAN—Foreign Investment and Growth in Vietnam, Thailand, Indonesia and Malaysia*, edited by Tran Van Hoa, pp. 87–97. Basingstoke: Macmillan, 1997.

Maitland, E. "Foreign Investors in Vietnam: An Australian Case Study". In *Vietnam Assessment: Creating a Sound Investment Climate*, edited by S. Leung, pp. 90–106. Singapore: Institute of Southeast Asian Studies, 1996.

Masuyama, S. and T. Tamao. "Vietnam's Participation in AFTA, APEC, and WTO and the Development of Export Industries by Foreign Direct Investment". In *Study on Economic Development Policy in the Transition Toward a Market-oriented Economy in Vietnam—Phase 2*, Ministry of Planning and Investment of the Socialist Republic of Vietnam (MPI) and Japan International Co-operation Agency (JICA) 2, pp. 67–82. Hanoi, 1998.

Mayer, T. and J.L. Mucchielli. "Agglomeration Effects, State Policies, and Competition in the Location of Japanese FDI in Europe". In *Research in Global Strategic Management*, edited by J.L. Mucchielli, pp. 87–116. Greenwich, Ct.: JAI Press Inc, 1998.

McCulloch, R. "New perspectives on Foreign Direct Investment". In *Foreign Direct Investment*, edited by K. A. Froot, pp. 37–53. Chicago: University of Chicago Press, 1993.

Mekong Project Development Facility (MPDF). *Vietnam's Undersized Engine: A Survey of 95 Larger Private Manufacturers*. Hanoi: MPDF, 1999a.

――――. *SMEs in Vietnam: On the Road to Prosperity*, Hanoi: MPDF, 1999b.

Meyer, K. *Direct Investment in Economies in Transition*. Cheltenham: Edward Elgar, 1998.

Meyer, S. and T. Qu. "Place-Specific Determinants of FDI: The Geographical Perspective". In *The Location of Foreign Direct Investment*, edited by M.B. Green and R.B. McNaughton, pp. 1–14. Aldershot, U.K.: Avebury, 1995.

Ministry of Finance of the Socialist Republic of Vietnam (MOF). *Vietnam Road Map for Tax Reduction to Implement ASEAN Free Trade Area*. Hanoi, 1999.

Moran, T.H. "Shaping a Future for Foreign Direct Investment in the Third World". In *Foreign Direct Investments*, edited by H.W. Singer, N. Hatti and R. Tandon, pp. 59–76. New Delhi: Indus Publishing Company, 1988.

Mosley, P. *Overseas Aid: Its Defence and Reform*. Brighton: Wheatsheaf Books, 1987.

Mundel, R.A. "International trade and factor mobility". *American Economic Review* 47 (1957): 321–35.

Mundle S. and B. van Arkadie. *The Rural-Urban Transition in Vietnam: Some Selected Issues*. Manila: Asian Development Bank, 1997.

Murphy, A. "Western Investment in East-Central Europe: Emerging Patterns and Implication for State Stability". *Professional Geographer 44*, no. 3 (1992): 249–59.

Narula, R. *Multinational Investment and Economic Structure—Globalisation and Competitiveness*. New York: Routledge, 1996.

National Political Publishing House (NPPH). *Documents of the 8th Party Congress Resolution*. Hanoi, 1996.

——. *Legal Documents Relating to Foreign Direct Investment in Vietnam*. Hanoi, 1999.

Nestor, C. "Foreign Investment and the Spatial Pattern of Growth in Vietnam". In *Uneven Development in Southeast Asia*, edited by C. Dixon and D.W. Smith, pp. 166–95. Brookfield, Vt.: Ashgate, 1997.

Ngo, T.H.H. "Hotel Chiefs Reject Proposals to Establish Fixed Room Rates". *Vietnam Investment Review*, no. 406 (1999).

Nguyen, A.T. "Firms Found Guilty of Overpricing". *Vietnam Investment Review*, no. 196 (1995).

——. "Tighter Standards Urged for Technology Transfer". *Vietnam Investment Review*, no. 248 (1996).

Nguyen, H. "Clothes-Makers Eye Extra EU Potential". *Vietnam Investment Review*, no. 415 (1999a).

——. "Hospitality Industry Has Severe Case of the Blues". *Vietnam Investment Review*, no. 380 (1999b).

Nguyen, H.S. "FDI and its Impacts on the Economy of Vietnam". *Asia-Pacific Economic Review*, no. 10 (1996b): 19–24.

Nguyen, N. "Indian Firm Backs Sugar". *Vietnam Investment Review*, no. 192 (1995).

Nguyen, N.C. "Made in Vietnam Computers on Sale". *Vietnam Investment Review*, no. 338 (1998).
———. "Fujitsu to Break the Billion Barrier". *Vietnam Investment Review*, no. 382 (1999c).
Nguyen, N.T., T.L. Ngo and P. Ho. "Restructuring of SOEs Toward Industrialisation and Modernisation in Vietnam". In *State-Owned Enterprise Reform in Vietnam—Lessons from Asia*, edited by C.Y. Ng, pp. 19–37. Singapore: Institute of Southeast Asian Studies, 1996.
Nguyen, Q.T. "Priority Areas to Attract Foreign Investment Capital to Vietnam: Present Conditions and Prospects". In *Economic Development and Prospects in the ASEAN—Foreign Investment and Growth in Vietnam, Thailand, Indonesia and Malaysia*, edited by Tran Van Hoa, pp. 98–112. Basingstoke: Macmillan, 1997.
Okada, E. "Obstacles to the Foreign Direct Investment to Vietnam—Implications for Resolving Conflict between High Economic Growth and Equality". In *Study on Economic Development Policy in the Transition Toward a Market-oriented Economy in Vietnam—Phase 1*, Ministry of Planning and Investment of the Socialist Republic of Vietnam (MPI) and Japan International Co-operation Agency (JICA) 3, pp. 57–66. Hanoi, 1996.
Organization of Economic Cooperation and Development (OECD). *Foreign Direct Investment and Economic Development—Lessons from Six Emerging Economies*. Paris: OECD, 1998.
Overseas Economic Co-operation Fund (OECF). *Debt Sustainability Analysis for Vietnam*. Tokyo: OECF, 1999.
Ozawa, T. "Foreign Direct Investment and Economic Development". *Transnational Corporations 1*, no. 1 (1992): 27–54.
Papanek, G.F. "Aid, Foreign Private Investment, Savings and Growth in Less Developed Countries". *Journal of Political Economy 81*, no. 1 (1973): 120–30.
Parry, T. *The Multinational Enterprise—International Investment and Host-Country Impacts*. Greenwich, Conn.: JAI Press, 1980.
Pham, H.M. and D. Forbes. "The ASEAN Free Trade Area and its Potential Impact on Vietnam's Economy". In *Development Dilemmas in the Mekong Sub-region*, edited by B. Stensholt, pp. 147–62. Melbourne: Monash University, 1996.
Phan, H.H. "Management of Foreign Direct Investment in Vietnam—Situation and Weaknesses". *Financial Review*, no. 4 (1998): 9–10.
Phan, V.T. and V.T. Nguyen. "Problems and Prospects of State Enterprise Reform, 1996–2000". In *State-Owned Enterprise Reform in Vietnam—Lessons from Asia*, edited by C.Y. Ng, pp. 3–18. Singapore: Institute of Southeast Asian Studies, 1996.
Pomfret, R. *Asian Economies in Transition—Reforming Centrally Planned Economies*. Brookfield, Vt.: Edward Elgar, 1996.

Popov, V.V. "Preparing the Russian Economy for World Market Integration". In *Regionalisation and Globalisation in the Modern World Economy—Perspectives on the Third Word and Transitional Economies*, edited by Jilberto and A. Mommen, pp. 86–127. New York: Routledge, 1998.

Rana, P.B. and J.M. Dowling. "The Impact of Foreign Capital on Growth: Evidence from Asian Developing Countries". *Developing Economies 25*, no. 1 (1988): 3–11.

Reinhardt, J. "Industrial Restructuring and Industrial Policy in Vietnam". In *Vietnam's Dilemma and Options—The Challenge of Economic Transition in the 1990s*, edited by M. Than and J.L.H. Tan, pp. 71–96. Singapore: Institute of Southeast Asian Studies, 1993.

Riedel, J. "Intra-Asian Trade and Foreign Direct Investment". *Asian Development Review 9*, no. 1 (1991): 110–46.

Robson, P. "Introduction: Transnational Corporations and Regional Economic Integration". In *Transnational Corporations and Regional Economic Integration*, edited by P. Robson, pp. 1–28. London: Routledge, 1993.

——. *The Economics of International Integration*, 4th edition. New York: Routledge, 1998.

Root, F. *International Trade and Investment*, 7th edition. Cincinnati: South-Western Publishing, 1994.

—— and A.A. Ahmed. "Empirical Determinants of Manufacturing Direct Foreign Investment in Developing Countries". *Economic Development and Cultural Change 27*, (1979): 751–67.

Rostow, W.W. *The Economics of Take-off into Sustained Growth*. London: Macmillan, 1963.

Rugman, A. "New Theory of Multinational Enterprise: An Assessment of Internationalisation Theory". *Bulletin of Economic Research 38*, no. 2 (1986): 101–18.

Sader, F. *Privatising Public Enterprises and Foreign Investment in Developing Countries 1988–93*. Washington D.C: World Bank, 1995.

Saigon Times Daily (STD). "Vietnam: Fresh Steps to Woo Investors". *Saigon Times Daily*, 26 March, 1999.

Saigon Times Magazine (STM). "Challenges Still Ahead". *Saigon Times Magazine*, 26 December, 1998.

Santiago, C.E. "The Impact of Foreign Direct Investment on Export Structure and Employment Generation". *World Development 15*, no. 3 (1987): 317–28.

Scaperlanda, A.E. and L.J. Mauer. "The Determinants of U.S. Direct Investment in the EEC". *American Economic Review 59*, (1969): 558–68.

Schnieder, F. and B.S. Frey. "Economic and Political Determinants of Foreign Direct Investment". *World Development 13*, (1985): 161–75.

Socialist Republic of Vietnam (SRV). *Vietnam: A Development Perspective*. Hanoi, 1993.

——. *Public Investment Program 1996–2000*. Hanoi, 1996.

Spulber, N. *Redefining the State—Privatisation and Welfare Reform in Industrial and Transitional Economies*. Cambridge U.K.: Cambridge University Press, 1997.

Sun, H. *Foreign Investment and Economic Development in China 1979–1996*. Brookfield, Vt.: Ashgate, 1998.

Svetlicic, M., P. Artisien and M. Rojec. "Foreign Direct Investment in Central and Eastern Europe: An Overview". In *Foreign Investment in Central and Eastern Europe*, edited by P. Artisien, M. Rojec and M. Svetlicic, pp. 3–15. New York: St. Martin's Press, 1993.

Tan, G. *The Newly Industrialising Countries of Asia*, 2nd edition. Singapore: Time Academic Press, 1995.

——. *ASEAN Economic Development and Cooperation*. Singapore: Times Academic Press, 1996.

Than, M. and J.L.H. Tan. "The Vietnamese Economy in Transition—Introductory Overview". In *Vietnam's Dilemma and Options—The Challenge of Economic Transition in the 1990s*, edited by M. Than and J.L.H. Tan, pp. 1–21. Singapore: Institute of Southeast Asian Studies, 1993,

Thirwall, A.P. *Growth and Development*, 5th Edition. London: Macmillan, 1994.

Tiusanen, T. *Post Communist Capitalism and Capital: Foreign Investors in Transitional Economies*. Commack, N.J.: Nova Science Publishers, 1993.

Todaro, Michael. *Economic Development*, 6th edition. Reading, M.A.: Addison-Wesley, 1996.

Tran, A.T. "FDI—Important Part of Vietnam's Economy". *Economic Development Review*, no. 92 (1998a): 23–5.

Tran, N.C. *Technological Capability and Learning in Firms: Vietnamese Industries in Transition*. Brookfield, Vt: Ashgate, 1999.

Tran V.T. "Future Japan Foreign Direct Investment in Vietnam". *Saigon Economic Times*, no. 9 (1998b): 37–9.

Transnational Corporations and Management Division "The Effects of Integration on the Activities of Transnational Corporations in the European Community: Theory and Empirical Tests". In *Transnational Corporations and Regional Economic Integration*, edited by P. Robson, pp. 99–123. London: Routledge, 1992.

United Nations (UN). *Looking Ahead—A Common Country Assessment*. Hanoi: UN, 1999.

United Nations Conference on Trade and Development (UNCTAD). *Regional Economic Integration and Transnational Corporations in the 1990s: Europe, North America and Developing Countries*. New York: United Nations, 1990.

――――. *Transnational Corporations as Engines of Growth.* New York: United Nations, 1992.

United Nations Development Program (UNDP). *Country Report.* Hanoi: UNDP, 1999.

United Nations Industrial Development Organisation (UNIDO) and Development Strategic Institute of Ministry of Planning and Investment of the Socialist Republic of Vietnam (DSI). *Medium-Term Industrial Strategy of Vietnam.* Hanoi, 1997.

――――. *Vietnam—Industrial Competitiveness Review.* Hanoi, 1999.

Vaitsos C.V. "The Process of Commercialisation of Technology in the Andean Pact". In *Transnational Corporations and Technology Transfer to Developing Countries*, edited by E.K.Y. Chen, pp. 197–228. New York: Routledge, 1994.

Vernon R. "International Investment and International Trade in the Product Cycle". *Quarterly Journal of Economics* 80, no. 2 (1966): 190–207.

――――. *Storm Over the Multinationals: The Real Issue.* Cambridge, Mass.: Harvard University Press, 1977.

Vietnam Economic News (VEN). "Eleven Years of FDI". *Vietnam Economic News*, 21 (1998).

Vietnam Investment Review (VIR). "Telstra—VNPT Together for 11 years". *Vietnam Investment Review*, no. 319 (1997).

Vietnam Investment Review (VIR). "Investors Applaud Moves to Promote Foreign Firms". *Vietnam Investment Review*, no. 348 (1998a).

――――. "Tech Transfer Details Spelt Out Two Years and 40 Drafts Later". *Vietnam Investment Review*, no. 353 (1998b).

――――. "Battling the JV Labour Blues". *Vietnam Investment Review*, no. 409 (1999).

Vietnam Net News (VNN). "Looking Back One Decade of Attracting Foreign Direct Investment: The Overall Picture". *Vietnam Net News*, 17 July 1999.

Vietnam Tourism Authority (VTA). <www.vietnamtourism.com>, 2000.

Wade, R. *Governing the Market: Economic Theory and the Role of Government in East Asian Industrialisation.* New Jersey: Princeton University Press, 1991.

Wells, L.T. "Investment Incentives: An Unnecessary Debate". *The CTC Reporter*, Vol. 22 (1986): 58–60.

――――. "Mobile Exporters: New Foreign Investors in East Asia". In *Foreign Direct Investment*, edited by A.K Froot, pp. 173–92. Chicago: University of Chicago Press, 1993.

Wheeler, D. and A. Mody. "International Investment Location Decision: The Case of US Firms". *Journal of International Economics* 33 (1992): 57–76.

White, H. "The Macro-Economic Impacts of Development Aid". *Journal of Development Studies* 28, no. 2 (1992): 163–240.

Wilmore, L. "The Competitive Performance of Foreign and Domestic Firms in Brazil". *World Development 14*, no. 4 (1986): 489–502.

Wimberley, D.W. "Investment Dependence and Alternative Explanations of Third World Mortality: A Cross-National Study". *American Sociological Review 55* (1990): 75–91.

——. "Transnational Corporate Investment and Food Consumption in the Third World: A Cross–National Analysis". *Rural Sociology 56* (1991): 406–31.

World Bank. *Vietnam—Economic Report on Industrialisation and Industrial Policies*, Washington D.C.: World Bank, 1995a.

——. *Vietnam—Poverty Assessment and Strategy*. Washington D.C.: World Bank, 1995b.

——. *World Development Report 1996—From Plan to Market*. Oxford University Press, 1996.

——. *Private Capital Flows to Developing Countries*. New York: Oxford University Press, 1997a.

——. *Vietnam Deepening Reform for Growth*. Washington D.C.: World Bank, 1997b.

——. *Vietnam Rising to the Challenge—An Economic Report*. Washington D.C.: World Bank, 1998.

——. *World Development Report 1998/99*. New York: Oxford University Press, 1999a.

——. *Vietnam—Preparing for Take-Off? How Vietnam can Participate Fully in the East Asian Recovery*. Washington D.C.: World Bank, 1999b.

Yannopolous, G. "Foreign Direct Investment and European Integration: The Evidence from the Formative Years of the European Community". *Journal of Common Market Studies* 28 (1990): 235–59.

Zhang X. "Foreign Investment Policy, Contribution and Performance". In *Foreign Direct Investment and Economic Growth in China*, edited by Y. Wu, pp. 11–41. Cheltenham, U.K.: Edward Elgar, 1999.

Index

A
agricultural sector
  competition 45
  FDI, effects 44
  participation 26
ASEAN countries
  technology transfer, source 71
ASEAN Free Trade Area (AFTA) 33
  Vietnam's commitment 127
Asia newly industrialized countries
  technology transfer, source 71
automobile industries, oversupply 34

B
balance of payments 41

C
capital, contributions 42
China, economic growth 15

D
defensive import-substituting investment 13
definitions
  foreign direct investment 4
dependency theory 8
dividends, foreign contribution 58
domestic enterprises, advantages 49
Dunning's Eclectic Theory 7

E
economic integration 13, 14, 127
employees
  shortage 116
  state-owned enterprises 51
  training enhancements 73
employment
European Community trade agreement 32

export performances
  regression analysis 136–40
  foreign invested projects 114, 115
export-oriented industrialization 12, 13; 79, 80–84
  FDI contribution 132

F
foreign currencies
  government policies 94
  outflow 56
foreign direct investment (FDI)
  allocation, regional 101–6, 128, 129
  comparative advantages 81
  definition 4
  differing viewpoints 1, 6–8, 130–34
  direct contribution 39, 40, 132
  factors affecting 29, 30, 32, 107
  forms 5, 25
  government, role 9, 122, 123
  government revenue, contribution 59
  gross domestic product, as percentage of 38
  growth 1, 131
  impact, indirect 43–5
  imports, impact on 54–7
  investment source, as 122–4
  mainstream view 7
  obstacles 34, 35
  poverty, alleviating 110–13
  projects, average size 24
  projects, salaries in 117, 118
  regression analysis 145–52
  stages 27, 28
  technology, source 70
foreign invested enterprises
  export structure 83

169

government policies promoting 84, 85
industrial capital 91
industrial output 78–82, 91
regional analysis 136–44
foreign invested projects
  employees, wages of 117
  workforce 114, 115
  performance 66, 67
foreign investments
  countries involved 83, 84, 105
  technology transfer 70–74
foreign investors, ownership advantages 33
foreign loans 57

G
garment industry, growth 88
geographic regions 98, 99
  economic indicators 100
  factors affecting FDI 107
  poverty 111
government policies 9
  FDI, attracting 129, 133
  foreign invested enterprises, promoting 84–7
  impact 93–5
  internalization 33
  government roles
  maintaining stability 14
  gross domestic product 19, 20
  FDI contribution 38, 62, 63
  industrial output structure 77

H
Harrod-Domar model 17
  problem 61
hotel industry, oversupply 34; 53
Hymer
  international organization theory 6

I
import substitution
  industrialization 11, 12, 87–92
  domestic market protection 93
imports
  FDI, impact 54–7
  old technology 74, 75
industrial capital outlay, growth 52
industrial indicators 72
industrial investment projects, priority 90

industrialization 76, 77, 78, 79
industrial output growth rate 51
industrial output structure 77, 79
industrial products 64, 65
inflation, reduction 22
International Monetary Fund (IMF)
  FDI, defining 4
international organization theory 6
investment, forms 25
investment incentive, impact 10, 11
iron and steel industry, growth 92

J
Japan
  overseas investments, reasons 31
joint ventures
  technology transfers 70

L
labour
  cheap 30
  government policies 118, 119
  skilled 116
labour force, educated 29, 117
Law on Foreign Direct Investment 70
  regional inequalities, addressing 106
Law on Foreign Investment 21
  amendments 32
  content 22
  implementation 35
local participation, requirement for 94
locational advantages 29

M
manufacturing sector
  FDI, impact 44, 45
market-oriented economy
  foreign direct investment, role 1

O
offensive import-substituting investment 14
overseas Vietnamese, investment by 40

P
population 19
poverty 110, 111
  alleviation 120
  FDI, impact of 112–7, 133

private sector
  participation in economy 26; 38, 47
  problems 48
production lines, automation 72

R
rationalized investment 14
regional development 98–101
  FDI allocation 101–6, 128, 132, 133
  FDI, impact 108
  industrial output 109
regression analyses
  data 137, 138, 142, 149, 150
  model 136, 137, 141, 142, 145–9
  results 86, 87, 94, 95, 138–40, 142–4, 151, 152
reorganization investment 14
Russia
  FDI, low level 16

S
salaries 117, 118
savings, domestic 37, 44
service industry, growth 105
skilled labour, shortage 116
social indicators 111
specialization ratio,
  improvement 92

state-owned enterprises
  autonomy 21
  characteristics, crucial 46
  employees 51
  FDI, impact 45
  performance 46

T
tariff protection 93
  reduction 125, 126
tax incentives, impact 10, 11, 93
tax rates, effect 86, 87
technology, transfer 69–74
  problems 74, 75
  policies 75, 76
textile industry, growth 32
trade agreement, European
  Community 32
trade policies, impact 11–14
transaction cost approach 6
transfer pricing 74, 75

V
Vernon's product life cycle model 6

W
wages 117, 118
waste processing systems 73
World Bank, projections 61